Fathers and Fathering

Also by Rev. Dr. Judith Larkin Reno

The Sacred Celebration Series
- *New Year Sacred Celebration: Find Your New Soul-Path*
- *Easter Sacred Celebration: Holy City Initiation*
- *Valentine's Day Sacred Celebration: The Deep Meaning of Love and Sex*
- *Mother's Day Sacred Celebration: The Divine Mother*
- *Fathers and Fathering: An Exploration*
- *Christmas Sacred Celebration: The Midnight Angel Procession*
- *Your Home Sacred Celebration: Your Home Angel*
- *Your Birthday Sacred Celebration: Find Your Soul-Path in Each Year*

The Love Relationship Series
- *Love is Made: The How-To Love Manual*
- *Healing the Broken Family: Skills for Renewal and Insight*
- *The Signature Wedding: Design Your Own Wedding Ceremony*

The Spiritual Championship Series
- *Reinventing God: God Discovery*
- *Divine Father—Your God: Deepening Your God Connection*
- *Divine Mother—Your Soul: Deepening Your Soul Connection*
- *Self-Interview: Using Your God Ladder for Self-Discovery*
- *A Mystic's View of War: Using the God Ladder for Clarity*
- *Elephants in Your Tent: Spiritual Support as a Mystic Survives Cancer*

Fathers and Fathering

An Exploration

Rev. Dr. Judith Larkin Reno

Wisdom Moon Publishing
2014

Fathers and Fathering:
An Exploration

Copyright © 2014 Judith Larkin Reno

All rights reserved. Tous droits réservés.

No part of this work may be copied, reproduced, recorded, stored, or translated, in any form, or transmitted by any means electronic, mechanical, or other, whether by photocopy, fax, email, internet group postings, or otherwise, without written permission from the copyright holder, *except for brief quotations* in reviews for a magazine, journal, newspaper, broadcast, podcast, etc., or in scholarly or academic papers, *when quoted with a full citation to this work.*

Published by Wisdom Moon Publishing LLC
San Diego, CA, USA

Wisdom Moon™, the Wisdom Moon logo™, *Wisdom Moon Publishing*™ , and *WMP*™ are trademarks of Wisdom Moon Publishing LLC.

www.WisdomMoonPublishing.com

ISBN 978-1-938459-33-7 (softcover, alk. paper)
ISBN 978-1-938459-39-9 (eBook)

LCCN 2014936146

TABLE OF CONTENTS

INTRODUCTION	i
MY JOURNEY OF DISCOVERY	1
CULTURAL IMAGES	4
MODERN DAD'S DILEMMA	11
FATHERHOOD EXPERIENCES	14
QUALITIES OF FATHERING	17
HEALTHY MARRIAGE	22
HEALTHY FAMILY	39
CHILD ABUSE	49
HEALTHY PARENTING	57
DAD'S PSYCHOLOGICAL LEGACY	69
EXPLORING YOUR FATHER	78
TAOISM'S GENDER MODELS	87
JUNG'S GENDER MODELS	94
YOUR SOUL AND YOUR SPIRIT	100
MALE ACTION-DERANGEMENT	103
SOCIETAL GENDER LIES	116
ESOTERIC GENDER MODELS	126
KABALA GENDER MODELS	141
JOSEPH, FATHER OF THE HOLY FAMILY	143
SKY FATHER AND EARTH MOTHER	149

INDIAN WEDDING BLANKET	**152**
THE FIRST FATHER'S DAY	**157**
CO-CREATION	**166**
THE WISE MAN AND THE WISE WOMAN	**173**
THE PARENT'S JOURNEY	**191**
HONORING FATHER	**195**
SPIRITUAL ADULTHOOD	**202**
FOR FURTHER STUDY	**205**

INTRODUCTION

THE AUTHOR

With a Ph. D. in Psychology and forty years of experience as a mystic, counselor, and teacher, Rev. Dr. Judith Larkin Reno offers a singular blend of insight. She embraces both Eastern and Western, ancient and modern, psychological and spiritual wisdom. She presents rare information from a lifetime of global travel and a wide variety of mystical traditions.

Rev. Dr. Reno's germinal thinking reveals uniquely original ideas and approaches to higher consciousness. She deepens your self-discovery and conscious living.

As an interfaith minister, Rev. Dr. Reno opens dimensional doorways between the worlds—earthly and divine. She empowers your advanced spirituality. In the hurly burly, soul-robbing life of secular society, Rev. Dr. Reno unites you with the holy, blessed ordinariness, and consecrated living.

As a spiritual cartographer, she provides maps, models, methods, and mentoring for enlightenment. Dr. Reno is a mystic who makes spiritual technologies user-friendly. Her profound God Ladder insights are a singular contribution to modern spiritual literature.

As a grandmother, Judith has "seen a lot of lightning" and lived to speak the story. Her life spans almost one-third of American history.

She shares unique, lived-wisdom—with practical solutions to life's complex problems.

Rev. Dr. Reno is Founder and President of Gateway University®, a school for the study of higher consciousness, outside of San Diego, California, where she enjoys teaching, counseling, and writing. She also enjoys her husband; family, and friends; playing the violin; and hiking in nature.

THE SERIES

Restore the holy to your holidays. The **SACRED CELEBRATION SERIES** shares the esoteric side of calendar holidays through the year. Sacred celebrations are soul vitamins. They strengthen your spiritual journey and refuel your love-tank each month.

Reading the entire series gives you an excellent spiritual education and increased esoteric knowledge. Each **SACRED CELEBRATION** book has companion audios to enrich your spiritual path. These books offer rare, mystical illumination helping you to consecrate daily life.

THE BOOK

FATHERS AND FATHERING: An Exploration examines the deep meaning of manhood and fathering. Rev. Dr. Reno shares her surprising adventures discovering healthy fathering and deep male-essence across a lifetime. Her insights are singular and fresh.

Today's culture presents a jumble of images regarding father. This book brings clarity to fathering, your childhood, healthy parenting, and internal self-parenting. You see the father's profound service to family life as well as the hazards of fathering.

Dr. Reno uncovers socially ignored internal gender-essences, as well as twisted social-roles, for both genders. She unveils gender history, presenting models of gender from the culture, psychology, and esoteric traditions. ***Fathers and Fathering*** explores the male principle inside each of us including its physical, emotional, mental, and spiritual aspects.

Fathers and Fathering

Every year on Father's Day, we reflect on father and our relationship with him. Fathering is rigorous and exhausting—even in the best of times. It is a time/labor intensive job that is often thankless. Through interactive questions and valuable information, you develop a deeper understanding of the men in your life—including your father, your internal male, and Divine Father.

Most importantly, you provide a healthy family for your own children. Many families are adrift in a sea of confusion. Families urgently need this book with its important skills and practical guidance for parenting, families, men/women, and fathering.

Governments and world leaders across the world demonstrate Rev. Dr. Reno's observation: "There's no adult in charge! Our leaders are adult-children, locked in immature behavior. Too many of them demonstrate arrested development from dysfunctional parenting."

Families are where children learn morality, respect for the law, love, relationship, and leadership. Without healthy families, civilization is at risk. Healthy fathering is essential, both personally and globally.

Humanity is at a choice-point. Are we evolving to embody soul or remaining action-deranged, egotistical children? Can we move from "me" to "we"—from power-games to co-creation, from arrested development to spiritual adulthood? Can we heal our broken father models? The essential dialogue is between adult/child, male/female, mom/dad earthly/divine archetypes. This conversation is inside each of us today.

> **This book is medicine for healthy fathering.**
>
> **It illumines gender wars and planetary confusion.**
>
> **It heals your parenting, your childhood, internal voices, and this moment in history.**

Fathers and Fathering provides specific remedies for healthy fathering and father-repair from your childhood. It helps you to decipher the puzzle-pieces of your life—including both male and female roles. Shining light on internal father, healthy male, and

Divine Father, it illumines the Wisdom Way going forward into the New Wisdom Age.

Come along with Rev. Dr. Reno as your expert guide on this adventure in self-discovery!

MY JOURNEY OF DISCOVERY

I've never been an ordinary woman—as hard as I've tried. As a mystic, I grew up hearing nursery rhymes about "The butcher, the baker, the candlestick maker," but never one about the mystic.

I had this stubborn, probing instinct for deep meaning. It wouldn't go away. Deep-essence just WOWed me. Color me different. I am a mystic.

Part of my journey of self-discovery was to find how I fit in here, not only as a mystic, but also as a woman. In order to learn what it means to be a woman, I had to learn what it means to be a man. They are notably distinct in this world of duality.

My journey to the essence of manhood led to the essence of fathering. I experienced a rich lifetime of deep and variegated esoteric, spiritual, and psychological study, two marriages, children, grandchildren, and years and years of "love experiences" in the dating game. Pretty exhausting stuff, some of it! However, well worth the trouble.

In the following chapters, I share the golden nuggets of my journey. Hopefully, it will save you some agony. Each step reveals a different aspect of manhood and thus fathering. Often, a boy becomes a man through fathering.

As a mystic and psychologist, I marvel at how life has built-in developmental mandates. Each stage of life provides its unique curriculum. The uncompromising limits of the baby demand that the father learn self-transcendence.

Through selfless service to his child, the magic of love recreates the boy into a man. Granted there are more hard-knocks than the magic wand would imply. The ride through parenting is not exactly "Poof! We have an adult!" In real-time, it might take decades (or lifetimes) after the baby is born. Regardless, the gift of parenting is one of life's greatest pinnacles.

My exploration of what it means to be male and father begins with cultural images. It ranges through psychology, Taoism, Kabala, Native American Indian shamanism, Christianity, and esoteric gender-models. I include my original thinking re-visioning the First Father's Day. I also share my discussions with Joseph in his fathering journey of the holy family.

I learned that you can't explore male without exploring female. And, the plot thickens! My deep-dive into gender culminates with my unique discoveries of internal gender-essences and their relationship with gender social-roles.

My research into the healthy family shocked me. I realized I had never seen one! Writing this book is an effort to change that and to lift the ignorance in our families regarding how to be happy and healthy. A rigorous task that only a grandmother can tackle!

I give you skills that work for happy and healthy parenting. I give you interactive questions to further your journey of self-discovery. I share the God Ladder with its profound wisdom solutions to gender wars, broken families, and evolving the Human Experiment through the Wise Man and the Wise Woman.

Prepare for some deep-diving into essence. This book is deep. Hey! I'm deep. I'm a mystic and a psychologist. We will fly high and dive deep together.

I am endlessly discovering the marvels of being human. In the pinnacle a-ha moments of my exploration into manhood and fathering, I'm reminded of T. S. Eliot's beautiful insight

> *We shall not cease from exploration, and the end of all our exploring will be to arrive where we started and know the place for the first time.*

Fathers and Fathering

My prayer for you is that through this exploration, you may see something as familiar as manhood and fatherhood through new eyes. May the chills and thrills of this magical life-ride unfurl your heart. May you receive full bounty of life's wonderment, as we explore together.

Judith Larkin Reno

CULTURAL IMAGES

To launch our exploration of the healthy male and fathering, let's play with the following questions and cultural clues. Much of what we learn about families and role models comes from movies and the media.

Who are some ideal fathers in our culture? Often we identify what we like, by learning what we don't like. List fathers you admire or dislike from movies, TV, literature, songs.

Here are some questions to catalyze your self-discovery and clarify your thinking.

- ➢ **What father images are portrayed in movies through the decades?**
    - The Victorian autocrat in *Life with Father*.
    - Jimmy Stewart as a good, but imperfect man in *It's a Wonderful Life*.
    - Gregory Peck's moral strength as Atticus Finch in *To Kill a Mockingbird*.
    - Robert De Niro's hard-working blue-collar dad in *A Bronx Tale*.
    - Martin Scorcese's corrupting gangsters in *Goodfellas*.
    - Dustin Hoffman fighting his liberated ex in *Kramer v. Kramer*.

Fathers and Fathering

- *Three Men and a Baby*, the male approach to baby-care.
- *My Life as a House*, an intimate, introspective of one man's experience of being male.
- Steve Martin in *Parenthood*. Fun and sweet.
- Brad Pitt's stern, brutal dad in *The Tree of Life*.
- *The Kids are All Right* (2011), toggling together of sperm-dad with same-sex parents and their children.
- George Clooney in *The Descendants* (2012), discovering the world of family that he had inadvertently abandoned in favor of work.
- Christopher Plummer coming out of the closet at 75 before relating to his son in *Beginners*.
- Robert Downey Jr. in *Due Date*.
- *Super 8*, two father's finally learning to embrace their children.
- *Winter's Bone*, dad as meth addict.
- *White Irish Drinker*, dad as violent alcoholic.
- *Somewhere*, dad as fame-driven, debauched actor."
- Adam Sandler's *That's My Boy!* (2012), with dad as a result of an inappropriate student-teacher union.
- *Beasts of the Southern Wild*, a father's savage training, preparing his daughter for life's storms after his death.
- Tom Hank's beautiful male-modeling to a culture much in need in *Extremely Loud, Incredibly Personal*. This inspiring exploration uncovers three generations of father-son relationships and depicts a truly healthy family.

In the overview of films, notice the messy mélange of father images. Do you think our culture is confused about fathering and what it is to be male?!

Reviewing earlier films, we see a progression from the rigid, idealized autocrats who wielded father's superior moral certitude in the 1800 and early 1900s, rolling through more recent male images with Cary Grant's charm, John Wayne's stoicism, and Humphrey Bogart's stubbornness.

Father/male images moved into the rebellious mid-century with Jimmy Dean's *Rebel without a Cause* (1955) to Steve McQueen's motor-cycle hero in *The Great Escape* (1963) and Paul Newman's chain-gang *Cool Hand Luke* (1967).

Dad's superiority deconstructed through subsequent decades of bad-dads, confused dads, legally-confronted dads, and morally ambiguous dads—not to mention sperm dads!

➢ **What father images are portrayed on TV through the years?**

- *Father Knows Best*. Dads in the 1950s were typically remote, at their jobs all day. They were autocratic in solving family problems when they got home at night. Moms were stereotypical homemakers, never stepping outside their family duties. They managed all the domestic chores—especially meals. The middle-class was newly invented. Suburban life was portrayed as the ideal.

- *Ozzie and Harriet*. The 1960s still depicted rigidly idealized families. However, it introduced a bit more laughter into family-life. The father-image was more a treasured fantasy, rather than reflecting real life.

- *Leave It to Beaver*. Dad still had all the wise answers. He was a guiding, god-like figure who could be relied upon to bring home the bacon. He was the patriarch and family's moral compass.

- *The Walton Family*. This sentimentalized and sweet portrayal from the 1970s showed a large farm-family facing hard times with moral fortitude.

- *Happy Days*. Fonzie's (Henry Winkler) leather jacket and motorcycle was edgy for 1970s. Fonzie was the likeable anti-hero as the new male. The Vietnam War splintered the iconic, remote, idealized dad/male image.

- *All in the Family*. Norman Lear showed the nation its own ridiculous bigotry through his Archie Bunker during the 1970s, a time of race-riots and women's lib.

Fathers and Fathering

- *The Brady Bunch.* Dad, Mike Brady was one of TV first stepfathers with his blended family of six kids.
- *Family Ties.* Both parents, Elyse and Steven Keaton, worked full-time. Both parents had an equal voice in running the household.
- *The Cosby Show.* He was a doctor. She was a lawyer. Suddenly, dad was no longer the sole provider in TV-land. Claire Huxtable demonstrated the wife as an equal to her husband, as first and second wave feminism integrated in the culture. Also, there was increased racial parity in TV programming.
- *Full House.* Bob Saggit's dad is hands-on, domestically involved in singly raising the kids, representing the newly constellated families of the 1980s.
- *Married with Children.* The deplorable dads began. Al Bundy was the anti-dad who would rather be anywhere than with his family.
- *The Simpsons.* Baby-man, Homer Simpson was belching, drinking, tripping, and being mothered by his wife, rather than parenting.
- *Family Guy.* Another idiot dad deconstructs the calcified patriarchal model.
- *Everyone Loves Raymond.* The dad is often a bungling caricature in this 1990s program, while Debra rationally holds things together. However, Ray tries. He is up against his parents' quintessential intrusiveness. The series repeatedly showcases a lack of healthy boundaries and psychological ignorance regarding healthy family-systems. However, the love is always redemptive.
- *Roseanne.* Brassy and bold, Roseanne and Dan are the working class family up-against often messy, hard reality, but bonded together with love. Plain talking and real are refreshing hallmarks of this series, reflecting the 1990s.
- *Ozzy Osbourne Reality Show.* Ozzy and Sharon's wildly dysfunctional parenting is unashamedly show-cased in the decade of the '00s.

- *Till Death.* Blatant, psychological honesty is a hallmark of today's TV family depictions.
- *Exes.* Reflects the contemporary divorce epidemic.
- *Modern Family.* ABC showcases the wide variety of contemporary families: the gay couple; the older man/younger woman; the emotionally-sensitive father who is counseled by his more mature children, in parent-child role reversals.
- *Parenthood.* NBC's shows the nurturing, stay-at-home dad and the high-powered, lawyer mom in the parenting role-reversals of 2010.
- *Dads.* Fox's 2013 portrayal of two generations of men living together rolls-out the responsible younger generation trying to do the right thing for their live-in dads who bungle forward in calcified splendor, while the younger men speak openly about sex and listen sensitively (occasionally) to women.

Today, in this time of freewheeling choices, there is a chaos of father images. However, as Jenna Goudreau writes in Forbes, "...primetime lineups offer a range of dads and family set-ups that, arguably, more accurately reflect modern fathers: breadwinners, nurturers, sages, bumblers, and, most importantly, real guys who want to be great fathers but don't always know what they're doing."

There's a refreshing honesty today. Dads are more willing to be individuals, real humans, and not phony idealizations. Rather than rigid stereotypes, there is increased openness to learning and growing through co-parenting. Today's dads have better work-home balance than previous generations. Importantly, today's dads are more connected and communicative regarding their feelings.

They are not just absentee figments of the child's imagination. They are more present, more willing to be wrong, and even occasionally willing to cry!

> **What father images are portrayed in music?**

The Rolling Stones list of the 10 most popular songs about dads reads like a trail of tears with its desperate estrangements. However, there still are some beautiful songs memorializing dad. What are your favorite songs about dad? Here are some popular songs:

Fathers and Fathering

- "Oh, My Papa" from the idealized 1950s.
- 1969, the Winstons sing "Color Him Father" about a super stepdad who cares for his seven step-kids.
- "Father and Son," with Cat Stevens' 1970s singing of the father's patience and the son's readiness to break away and individuate.
- 1972, the Temptations "Papa Was a Rolling Stone" portrays a lazy womanizer.
- "Cat's in the Cradle," Harry Chapin's 1974 story of the father who is too busy for the son; then reversing roles when the father is older and ready to bond.
- 1980, John Lennon's "Beautiful Boy (Darling Boy)" when Lennon left his career to become a full-time dad, after completely abandoning his first son.
- Johnny Cash's "A Boy Named Sue" hi-lights dad's tough love.
- Country music is filled with songs about dads, including George Strait's moving "Love Without End, Amen."
- Phil Collin's 1989 ballad "Father to Son."
- Will Smith's 1997 beautiful "Just the Two of Us."
- Eric Clapton's 1998 "My Father's Eyes" explores the compound grief of not knowing his father and losing his young son in an accident.
- 2004, Paul Westerberg's "My Dad" is a warm tribute.
- Paul Overstreet's 2005 "Seeing My Father in Me."
- Mike and The Mechanics' "The Living Years" about the loss of father.
- Loudon Wainwright's beautiful "Everything She Knows I Taught Her" and his "Being a Dad."

> **What father figures, beyond your own, influenced your growing-up?**
- In your extended family?

- In your town or neighborhood?
- At school?
- Identify both the ones you admired and those that you disliked.

➢ **What father figures do you currently admire in your circle of friends?**

MODERN DAD'S DILEMMA

In cave man days, if you didn't like someone you could hit him or run away. You could externalize your feelings. However, in today's workplace of bureaucracy and business offices, it's illegal to hit your boss. If you run away, you lose your job.

You end up internalizing your emotions. Some researchers describe a fight, flight, or fear response. Fear can internalize your natural response to fight or flee, leaving you frozen in paralysis. Anger is another popular internalization.

In caveman days, emotions were out front. A father could stand and fight, or lead the family flight to safety—actively demonstrating his love for his family. He could physically act out his love by defending and protecting his family from external enemies. This proved his manhood to himself and to his tribe.

In modern times, a father can't act on his instinctual fight or flight response to protect his family. This creates pressure, anxiety, and separation from his natural self and from others.

Men have great amounts of testosterone. They are hormonally wired for action. Unless he has a strong exercise program, today's man's energy gets unnaturally short-circuited and internalized by working at a desk all day.

In addition, he is unnaturally separated from his family by modern demands of earning a living. In agrarian times, families lived and worked together. Father was visible and connected to the family. The natural male-mode of being was vibrationally installed in his son, as the two worked side by side. Manhood was modeled and non-verbally passed to the next generation of men.

In the Information Age, long hours at the office often make the modern dad invisible to his family. He may become an anonymous, distant, mythical figure to children who only see him a few hours a week.

Children get the message that dad's work is more valuable than they are. A child may unconsciously feel shamed by the lack of time father spends with him. Children can feel angered by dad's apparent shunning.

Society often locks the father into anti-family behavior, enduring long office hours, family alienation, and family deprivation in the name of the money-god.

It is an unnatural act for the father to leave his family as a way to demonstrate his love. He may feel like an outsider to the ones he loves most. He may also feel used, angry, and martyred. Fathers can endure agonizing loneliness, bearing the weight of primary bread-winner for the family.

A woman still only earns seventy-seven cents on a man's dollar for equal work. With only twenty of the Fortune 500 companies owned by women and less than twenty percent of the Congress female, there is a long way to go for gender parity in our nation. As long as gender apartheid continues, fathers bear an unfair financial burden in the family.

Because of his unavailability to the family, father may have few relationship skills. Society gives him a pay check for leaving his family—not for developing love skills. Healthy relationship skills require rigorous attention and development.

Relationship skills include both listening and speaking regarding intimate feelings. Skills include healthy:

> Boundaries and limits; entitlement; self-interview; objective naming skills; truth-telling; communication; active-listening with empathy; confrontation; impulse control; enlistment skills; and conflict resolution.

Fathers and Fathering

That's a lot! If a man is rewarded by society for being a non-relational bread winner, it may be challenging for him to develop these complex intimacy skills.

Is it easier to talk to your mother or your father? In general, people say that it is easier to talk to mom than to dad. Society doesn't motivate Dad to explore his feelings.

Self-awareness requires deep courage and time for reflection. In today's crazy-busy, accelerated world, it may be difficult to create even an hour a day for quiet time. The overwhelming, external assault of schedules, duties, and sheer information creates an avalanche. It fractures the self in an act of societal violence.

In this world of smoke and mirrors, the father is asked to leave his family every day to earn a living. Then, he is criticized for not having family relationship skills. Dad is in a double-bind.

FATHERHOOD EXPERIENCES

Exploring the experience of fatherhood, I asked some fathers the following questions. Here are there responses.

How did fatherhood change you?

- Albert became more protective. He felt an obligation to his child. He wanted to guide his child.
- Gary quit golfing.
- Trevor, "It almost killed me. It was the most exhausting, impossible thing I ever did. I almost went crazy. I don't know how I survived."
- Harry, "I don't have a clue."

What is the experience of fathering like?

- Ben raised four children. He said, "It's a hard life. I would never do it again. There are so many mouths to feed. It's a lot of duty and hard work. The good part is when the child grows up. Relief from pain when the child grows up is the only joy."
- Bill was a step-father for a year and half. It was rough, but he'd do it again. The kids acted out and were called in by the school principal. The police called once. Bill remembered his own childhood when he misbehaved. His friends were wild. He didn't think they'd live beyond eighteen. But they ended up becoming

responsible adults. Parenting helped Bill surrender his judgment. He says, "Parenting is difficult. But difficulty helps us grow. We wouldn't be here if we hadn't overcome difficulty."

- Mark describes fathering. He saw himself reflected in the demands he placed on his son. He had too many expectations. He said, "When the child doesn't behave the way you want, you have to deal with your expectations and surrender them." Mark's growth and self-discovery came through parenting. His self-confidence grew. But he said, "When the kid is obnoxious, the father suffers. The father has to surrender his need to be right and his pictures of how it's supposed to be." Mark's son played soccer. His son's ability to be aggressive and participate in the game was not what Mark wanted. Mark felt anger when his son didn't match his expectations. Mark learned to accept his son just as he was.

- Steve, "I couldn't wait until the kids left and I could have my house and my life back. It felt like an alien invasion."

- Aiden, "My wife flipped out and left me alone to raise our son. I had no idea what I was doing. I prayed. And, I prayed. It's been 15 years and I still haven't been on a date."

- Harry, "The kids turned out the opposite from me. I did my best. I paid the bills. I stuck it out until they all reached 18. Then, I left. It was like God's bad joke—a nightmare."

- John, "At first, there was this little miracle in the house. It was awesome. Then, more came. I was out-numbered. They didn't leave. They still won't leave. They go on forever."

- Greg, "I wanted to be like my father. I thought that was what to do. It didn't work."

- Rob, "Fathering is not about the parent. It's about unconditional love. You give up your life so you can show your child the right way. There's no time for bars and clubs and fantasy world. It's a messed-up world out there. We need to be careful. I meet my son's friends and their parents. If the parents use, the kids think it's OK. It's a full-time job being a father, 24/7. But there's no greater reward than raising my boy. There's nothing so exciting as seeing him grow and prosper. Absent parents miss that. It fills your heart with love and memories. All the pain and suffering is worth it."

- Joel, "I panicked when my first child was a boy. I thought, I'll have to take him camping, teach him fishing and baseball. I can't do any of that stuff. My son taught me how to be a father."
- Vince, "I'm the family body guard. I'm like a watch-dog. I keep them safe. They need me."
- Kenny, "My son taught me to be a man."
- Douglas, "Instead of buying my kids everything they wanted, when the money ran out, I learned to tell them 'I love you.' In the long run, the love is more valuable than the stuff."

While some fathers had healthy experiences, many seemed lost in a wilderness of confusion. The following exploration of healthy fathering provides a map through that wilderness."

QUALITIES OF FATHERING

ESSENTIAL ELEMENTS

What are the essential qualities of healthy fathering regardless of time in history? Here is some research on healthy fathering:

- The father defines the limits and the law.
- He defends healthy boundaries and protects the child's entitlement.
- Father is warrior, protector, and defender.
- He stands for justice.
- He is an authority figure.
- Father's duty is to stand and to protect his family.
- His strength defends the family, keeping it safe—both in emergencies and in daily life.
- He demonstrates the ability to act and to assert yourself.
- He embodies strength, safety, and security.
- He is a strength-giver.
- He is a knowledge-keeper.
- He provides mentoring and guidance.

- He is a healthy role model to look up to and to copy.
- Father provides a safe place for the child to grow and to develop.
- Fathering requires sacrifice, selfless-service, and love.
- Father embodies duty.
- Father is the purveyor of the adult archetype.
- Father teaches the family how to have fun, to balance work and reward.
- He demonstrates honesty and a healthy work-ethic.

Women marvel at men's physical strength and power. Men have extra testosterone, size, upper body muscles, and skeletal power. They can lift and move objects like gods. They effortlessly reach high places that women struggle to touch. Their deep voices are commanding.

THE CHILD'S GOD

To a tiny child, the father, with his many powers and vast dominion, is like a god. The child psychologically internalizes dad's example of manhood. However, physical manhood is much easier to achieve than psychological manhood.

If your dad didn't fulfill the above list of essential qualities, they may be lacking inside you. These qualities may be twisted, unclear, or deranged (put out of arrangement, disordered, imbalanced) in some way.

Without a good father-model to make it safe for you to grow up, you can become an endless child, lost in arrested development. You may never go through the healthy developmental tasks of each stage in life. You may never reach the fullness of mature living.

If you suffered bad-dad, you may psychologically polarize his qualities. You may over-express or under-express them, pushing-off from his example. You may oppositionalize from dad's toxic model, determined not to become like him.

Or, you could unconsciously imitate him, walking through life robotically without access to your authentic self. In addition to lacking healthy selfhood, if you suffered bad-dad, you may recreate difficult father figures in your daily life.

Whatever your unconscious choices are, dad is still running your life. Until you awaken from the hypnotic trance of your childhood, you don't have access to your authentic self and healthy choices.

INTERNALIZED DAD

Whatever you experienced of childhood, dad gets internalized as part of your psychological terrain. This in turn creates your external life.

Children invent their selfhood from dad's model—for better or worse. Some kids duplicate bad-dad. Others become his opposite.

For example, if you perceived your dad as a spineless worm, you may over-achieve determined not to be like him. Or, you might duplicate him with your "couch and slouch" persona.

Conversely, if your dad were a dictator, you may adopt the opposite, laissez-faire, carefree, care-less attitude—in your determination not to be like him. If you duplicate dictator dad, you might be controlling, needing to win and to dominate.

In addition to designing your selfhood, your father determines how you father your internal child. Look at the way you self-parent. In your Inner Village, do you self-parent your inner voices in a healthy way?

Use the above list of fathering qualities to assess the fathering you received. How is your childhood experience currently affecting you?

> ➢ Is there a pattern of victim or tyrant issues recurring in your life or in your head?

> ➢ Is there a dictator running your internal scripts? Are you brutally self-critical? Do you self-crucify? Do you always feel guilty, even when it's not your fault?

> ➢ Is your primary internal voice a tyrant? Demanding that you work harder? Do you see life as a chore? A war zone? Are

you always pushing to achieve, to get more, to do more, to "do a good job"? Is there never enough money?

➢ Or do you go to the opposite extreme, with no one in charge? Do you lack internal filters, living in complete self-indulgence? Do you indulge in revenge eating when life gets tough. Do you over eat? Over sex? Over gamble? Over buy? Over consume? Are you dependent on drugs, alcohol, caffeine, or cigarettes for your "happiness"? Do you lack good impulse control? Do you lack delayed-gratification skills?

➢ Is your primary internal voice an escapist? Stuffing your emotional pain with food? Distracting with endless pleasures? Are you addicted to media and/or video-games.

➢ Do you have boundary and entitlement issues? Do you stand-up and assert yourself? Too much? Too little?

➢ Do you have authority issues with teachers or whoever is "in charge"? Do you hate the government? Do you overly identify with revolutions? Are you frequently complaining about the law and "the rules"? Do you repeatedly get in disputes with doctors or nurses?

➢ Do you feel unsettled around police? On the freeway, when you see highway patrol, do you feel guilty for no reason? Do you frequently feel unsafe in life?

➢ How do you feel about the law? Intimidated? Anxious? Panicked? Offended? Invaded? Defiant? Furious? Destructive? Hostile?

➢ Are you paralyzed by inaction when you have to take care of yourself? Is it difficult to prepare an emergency kit and an evacuation plan? Does life overwhelm you?

If you answered yes to any of the above questions, you may have suffered toxic parenting as a child. You may have unresolved father issues that require digestion.

For deeper self-interview, see the following chapter *Exploring Your Father* with its *Fathering Questionnaire*.

POWER RETRIEVAL

The value of identifying bad-dad is not to blame him. We are all broken here, in the human journey. Everyone has a front and a back on a plane of duality, with both good and bad features.

Rather, the victory is in naming your childhood journey so you can be clear about it and retrieve your power from it. Once the light of consciousness turns-on, you can see how you recreate bad-dad's mistakes by your own self-perpetration—internally and externally.

Voilà! Then, *you can retrieve power that you lost in childhood.* You can't clean the mess in the room until you turn-on the light and see the mess. Once you clearly see your childhood journey, you can change the parts that don't serve you today.

LEARNING WHAT IS NORMAL

When you suffer dysfunctional parenting in childhood, you don't know what normal is. Each child assumes his childhood is the norm, just like everyone else experiences.

Sadly, the rules of normalcy may be opposite from your childhood programming. As you awaken, you may agonize. You may be shocked to realize your family was dysfunctional. One person described her awakening, "I was horrified and disbelieving when I learned what healthy normal is."

You may grieve as you relinquish old family illusions, fantasies, and idealizations. When long-cherished family figureheads and beliefs reconfigure, you may experience betrayal, anger, and loss. Establishing a healthy normal inside you requires time, attention, and hard work.

However, as you learn what healthy normal is, you are released from Pain Jail. You experience the freedom and natural ease of your true-self.

You then can be a healthy parent—not only to your inner child—but also to your family of creation.

HEALTHY MARRIAGE

Many fathers don't have a clue regarding healthy fathering, because they have never seen one! In fairness, neither has anyone else. It was in the 1980s before there was awareness in the general population about the dynamics of functional and dysfunctional families. Before that, no one knew what normal was!

Some studies say ninety-five percent of families are dysfunctional. Over fifty percent of marriages fail. Family problems often spawn addiction, mental illness, and crime. There is a shocking paucity of healthy parenting in America today. Indeed, there is an epidemic of dysfunctional families. This is a tragic legacy to leave our children.

If you can assess your original family dynamics, you gain insight to your own self-development. Then, you won't internalize a toxic childhood dad in your internal self-talk and self-parenting.

You can identify mistakes that were made, so you don't repeat them with your own children. Use the following chapters to gain skills and insight. Heal the past and build a healthy future for yourself and your family.

See my books *Healing the Broken Family: Skills for Renewal and Insight* and *Love is Made: The How-To Love Manual.* These books are also packed with valuable parenting skills, condensed from across my lifetime of counseling, teaching, and making mistakes in my personal life!

ESSENTIAL ELEMENTS

I asked a random sample of people, "What great marriages do you admire? What do you think makes a healthy marriage?" People responded quizzically. They paused and couldn't come up with much.

One person gave a deep answer. She said, "How can we have great marriages when no one has been raised by a healthy adult?! Most of us are adult-children, raised by parents who were adult-children."

Parents model behavior that is unconsciously copied when the child becomes a parent. Therefore, it is vitally important to consciously learn about healthy marriage and parenting. Use the following information to strengthen your healthy parenting skills. These valuable tools also help you to forgive any mistakes that were made in your childhood.

To begin, it's important to know that healthy marriage is characterized by:

- Respect
- Trust
- Commitment
- Honesty
- Good communication
- Shared core-values
- Best friends
- Humor

10 SKILLS FOR HEALTHY SELF AND RELATIONSHIP

When a marriage is healthy, a family is healthy. The following skills are modeled and automatically transfer to the child. These ten basic skills create healthy selfhood and relationship.

1. **Healthy boundaries.** Boundaries are limits. They show what is

yours, mine, and ours. With healthy boundaries, no one is enmeshed or walled-off—overly involved or too distanced. It is important to know your limits. Your power of "No" sets healthy limits. Your comfort zone defines your healthy boundary. It protects your healthy entitlement.

2. **Fair entitlement.** Know what is rightfully yours and what is due to you. When you have healthy limits and self-value, there is balanced give-and-take in your relationships. You understand what is fair and reasonable. Anger often signals a loss of fair entitlement or a boundary infraction. Healthy entitlement ensures that you do not indulge in codependent giving; nor allow anyone to abuse you. You don't give from an empty cup; nor do you bite a giving hand.

3. **Self-interview skills.** In healthy self-interview, you continuously run a feedback-loop to your body, emotions, mind, and spirit. You report your pain and pleasure from each domain. Through self-monitoring, you gain self-knowledge of your physical needs, your emotional wound-triggers, your false beliefs, and your unchanging spiritual connection. You use healthy communication skills to report your experiences—physical, emotional, mental, and spiritual—to your partner, including both positive and negative information. You objectively name your emotions as they arise. You use healthy release and resolution skills for your emotions. See the chapter on *Healthy Parenting* for skills on naming and resolving shadow emotions in *Naming Emotions*.

4. **Truth-telling skills.** You honor your experience—physical, emotional, mental, and spiritual. Acknowledging zones of public and private safety, you speak both to yourself and to others of your feelings, appetites, desires, likes, dislikes, beliefs, limits, and wishes. You practice self-observation and owning your shadow journey without shaming yourself or others. You value honesty and integrity as part of intimacy. True intimacy mandates the vulnerability of truth-telling.

5. **Communication skills.** You have the courage to report what you see, feel, hear, know, and experience without polarizing your partner. You practice speaking from your heart and from an "us" space, while being honest about your shadow experience. You use naming skills rather than blaming. You say "I feel..."

rather than "You did..." You value being non-judgmental and objective.

6. **Active-listening skills.** You name and reflect what you hear your partner say—in the moment, without judging or editing. You listen with your heart, with empathy. You validate your partner's experience, first. Then, you share your own experience.

7. **Healthy confrontation skills.** You try not to polarize, shame, or oppositionalize your partner. Using "I" statements is less polarizing than making "you did..." accusations. You give your power away if you make your partner the source of your unhappiness. You practice naming rather than blaming. There is a subtle energy difference between the two. Blaming is toxic, overly intense, judgmental, and shaming. It is polarized. Naming is objective, clear, empty, and non-judgmental. It is non-polarized. To navigate difficult subjects, you use **The Sandwich Technique: Good news. Bad news. Good news.**

8. **Impulse control.** Violence and over-excitement are never appropriate. The ability to hear "No" and to delay gratifying your needs without taking offense is a valuable intimacy skill. It is also a sign of healthy adulthood. Anger must be carefully expressed and contained. Use vigorous physical exercise to transmute excessive, toxic, emotional energy.

9. **Enlistment skills.** You give your partner the information s/he needs to serve your needs. You enlist your partner to help you. You don't assume your partner knows what you want or need. It is your job to take care of yourself by enlisting the support of others. You schedule your enlistment time carefully when no one is tired, hungry, horny, or distracted. You calendar private time without interruptions.

10. **Conflict resolution skills.** You identify each point of view fairly and judiciously. You take each view seriously. There are five ways to resolve a conflict: 1) We do it your way. 2) We do it my way. 3) We do it your way, followed by my way. 4) Vice versa. 5) Or, we compromise. You continue your discussion until everyone is satisfied.

HEALTHY BOUNDARIES

Boundaries set the limits of healthy behavior. Healthy boundaries are defined by what is legitimately yours, mine, and ours.

In marriage, infidelity defines the limits of healthy love. Drug abuse and violence are additional markers delineating unhealthy relationship. In fact, any kind of abuse is a boundary violation including: physical, emotional, mental, financial, or spiritual abuse. These are all deal-breakers for marriage.

Healthy boundaries require clear agreements. Make sure your actions are honest. Is your agreement aligned with healthy boundaries and fair entitlement? Are you giving beyond your comfort range? Are you taking too much?

Work for a balance of give-and-take. When only one person gives and the other person receives, there are unhealthy boundaries.

If you are giving from an empty cup, it is false-giving. You have given beyond healthy limits. Healthy giving is joyful and easy. It doesn't involve suffering, martyrdom, and pain.

In general,

- Women tend to over-extend personal boundaries until there is nothing left for themselves. They enmesh their boundaries, confusing their sense of self with their beloved.
- Men tend to wall-off to and retreat from love as perceived invasion. They can feel suffocated by a simple request from a woman.

While women may tend to have too few boundaries, men can erect too many barriers against intimacy. Both extremes of codependent giving and isolating can reflect unhealthy boundaries.

YOURS, MINE, AND OURS

Healthy boundaries are defined by: What is yours, mine, and ours?

A healthy parent teaches the child to hold her hand to her chest saying "This is mine." Then, holding her hand with the palm facing outward, she says "That is yours." The child needs a tangible, physical anchor when learning her healthy entitlement and boundaries.

"What is ours?" is a more sophisticated skill that requires "walking in the other person's moccasins," then figuring out what is fair and equitable—both to the other and to yourself.

Developing healthy boundaries requires consistent parental guidance asking the child repeatedly: What is yours? What is mine? What is ours? Where is the boundary between the two? What benefits me? What benefits you? What do you truly desire? What do you feel? What do you think?

Honest self-interview reveals healthy limits and entitlement.

ENTITLEMENT

Entitlement is self-value. It is basic to defining selfhood. Knowing your value is essential self-esteem. Without healthy entitlement, victim/tyrant scripts can prevail, in your self-talk or your relationships.

Healthy entitlement skills involve continuously asking: "What is fair to me?" You discover that by rigorous self-interview: "What do I feel? What do I want? What do I desire? What do I deserve?"

Entitlement is self-advocacy. You must speak for your rights. Otherwise, you send a signal that you have no interest, desires, or value. Don't expect others to automatically understand what is yours and what you treasure. You must communicate your desires.

If you self-erase, others will erase you. Staying connected with your self-value and entitlement ensures fairness.

SELF-INTERVIEW SKILLS

Each partner's job in marriage is self-interview. You are responsible for identifying your needs and limits, your likes and dislikes. It is your responsibility to speak of them to your partner.

Don't assume your partner knows what you want. It's not fair to expect your partner to read your mind. Your partner only knows what you tell her.

Practice continually scanning each level of your being for information: physical, emotional, mental (your beliefs), and spiritual. Staying present with yourself allows you to be present in your love relationship.

To self-interview, imagine that you are a reporter, relaying information from the frontlines of your body, emotions, mind, and spirit. Continually ask: What am I feeling now? Then, listen to the response from your physical body, your emotions, your beliefs, and your God connection. Report the answers to your conscious self and to your partner, when it's appropriate.

Ask yourself: What do I want? What do I need? Often, they are different. Be ruthlessly honest with yourself. Run fearless self-interviews continually throughout the day to stay present.

Here are some self-interview questions:

- What **physical** appetites, desires, likes, dislikes, am I feeling? Am I hungry, horny, or tired?

- Review your **3 basic shadow emotions**. Am I feeling angry, sad, or afraid?

- What do I want, desire, and need right now? Don't ask "What should I want?" Rather, ask "What do I honestly want and need to feel happy?" Say: I feel ___. I want ___. I need ___.

- What do I **believe** right now? What am I being asked to believe? Are the two congruent? What are my moral values? Are my actions aligned with my beliefs?

- What is the right thing to do in this situation? Am I acting in accord with Goodness, including both love and truth—both for myself and for the other? Does this action *feel* right? Does my conscience feel clear? If not, wait until you have clarity.

- Is this honest giving? Do I really have this to give without undue suffering?

Self-interview involves continuous self-monitoring and self-awareness, using objective naming skills. Feelings don't lie. They keep you aligned with Truth and right-action. See the chapter on *Naming Emotions* for a deeper description of these skills.

Here are some additional tips for healthy self-interview:

> - Accurately name your experience: physical, emotional, mental, and spiritual.
> - Clearly discern what is yours, mine, and ours.
> - Clearly perceive healthy entitlement and fair limits.
> - Take responsibility for your own negative feelings, repression, over-expression, projection, unhealthy reactions, and unfairness.

Parents teach children healthy self-interview skills when they ask the child to report the good news/bad news of the day. Just asking yourself or your child "What were the highs and lows today?" keeps you in touch with healthy self-interview. It keeps you up to date with yourself.

TRUTH-TELLING

Impeccable honesty is essential in self-interview. Without a ruthless, fearless self-inventory, you are living a lie. If you fudge on your self-interview, you are only fooling yourself.

Telling the truth to your partner is the foundation of healthy relationship. Without trust, there is no relationship. You are in relationship with an imagined fantasy.

Confess when you are wrong. Ask your partner for forgiveness. Ask what you can do to repair the damage.

Truth-telling builds trust. The trust bridge is one of your most valuable assets in marriage. It must be maintained.

ZONES OF INTIMACY

There are three zones of intimacy: **personal, intimate, and public**. They expand from private to public, in concentric circles, with you at the center. Each zone has a different rule-book for healthy communication and boundaries. For example, what you say in public is not what you might say to your beloved or in the privacy of your own thoughts. You don't undress in public, but you do with your beloved.

The most naked truth is the one you tell yourself in your private self-talk, your internal self-interview. This is the closest circle, your **personal zone**. Here, the rule is raw truth: "I hate the way he chews." "I wish she'd lose some weight." These scripts are often brutally honest and not ready for primetime with your beloved.

"Love is made" as I say in my book by the same title. Your job is to make love, like fresh bread, each day. You must not intentionally alienate your partner. Hurtful truths are kept in the personal zone, until the right time for careful translation into your beloved's world.

Some toxic truths can be transmuted internally through meditation and self-reflection. Other times, you transmute negativity by reframing the situation.

For example, a nun transmuted her toxic truth when she loathed her partner sitting opposite her at the daily wash-tub. Her partner thoughtlessly splashed water all over everything and everyone. In meditation, the frustrated nun's Soul said, "What would Jesus do in this circumstance?" The next day, while scrubbing the clothes, the nun imagined that her partner was Jesus. She reframed the annoying splashes into holy baptismal sprinklings. She emerged from wash-duty fully consecrated by her holy partner. She even looked forward to her daily baptisms!

The poet said, "Life has loveliness to sell." Everything in life has its price. The **intimate zone** is with your beloved, your partner. This zone must be managed with care, love, and kindness. That is the price of a loving relationship.

To insure love, process your raw feelings, privately. Identify your wound-triggers and do emotional-release work. To focus your emotions ask yourself: When she does ____, I feel ____.

Transmute as much toxic energy as you can. Use fearless self-interview and reframing skills. Discover how your partner is serving you. What are you trying to learn through the negative feelings?

Fathers and Fathering

Before you speak to your beloved, find the heart of compassion to center yourself. Put yourself in the other's shoes. Unify with your partner. Communication is most effectively done from a soft heart-space.

Translate your private zone into your beloved's world. Find acceptable words that he can hear. Package your feelings so your partner can empathize with you. Carefully construct a word-bridge from your world into his.

Use colorful, concrete word-pictures to describe how you feel, such as: Food Devil, Nazi Brain Police, La-La Land. Describe "the movie in your mind." Imagine you are casting the film. Give the major players—you and your beloved—endearing titles or names that reveal the problem.

In your pre-game rehearsal, exaggerate characters for effect as if you were creating a cartoon of your life. It helps if you can stretch your melodramatic tale of woe to the point that you laugh about your own story.

Use humor, more humor, and more humor. Don't take yourself too seriously. Create cartoon pastiches of your bunglings—both your own and your partner's. Mentally referencing old cartoons of Bugs Bunny, the Roadrunner, et al. with their hair-raising capers can help you to reframe your pain into life's larger perspective.

Now, you are ready for primetime communication with your beloved. Buffer your negative report by balancing it with something you admire about your partner. Use your Love Sandwich: Good news. Bad news. Good news.

After you communicate, receive your partner's feedback. It may not be what you would like to hear. Work with it, back and forth, communicating your feelings and hearing your partner's experience.

At some point in all relationships, you accept that no one is perfect and that that is the price of love. That is mature, adult love.

The **public zone** is less complex than the intimate zone. Basically, keep your clothes on and stay out of jail! In the public zone, no one has the right to know your private business. The rules for healthy communication become more insulated, distanced, protected, and censored. Find what is appropriate and comfortable for you.

Of the three zones, the only unfiltered zone is your private self-interview.

HEALTHY COMMUNICATION

Plan your communications with your beloved for success. Make an appointment to discuss important issues. Choose a time when no one is hungry, tired, horny, or distracted. Agree not to take phone calls or interruptions during your discussion. Find a quiet place.

Healthy communication is done with respect, love, and humor; not as power struggle, ego battle, or control issue. Check to see if your heart is soft during communication and confrontation. Engender support by speaking in a respectful way that your partner can hear. Be humble.

With healthy communication, confrontation, and resolutions skills, everyone gets her/s needs met. There are no martyrs or tyrants. Discuss the subject until every question is answered and every need is satisfied. Dr. Amy Guttman, President of the University of Pennsylvania, says "Familiarity breeds attempt." Keep communicating until you reach resolution.

> **The sign of a healthy love relationship is not that you never argue; but that you argue to completion. Unhealthy marriages have the same argument for years because issues never get resolved.**

It's not fair to your partner if you run from the room before resolving your conflict. Only leave the room if tempers escalate.

It takes courage to become vulnerable and to confess your true feelings. Often emotions aren't what you wish they were. It can be difficult to own negative feelings and to speak of them.

Set healthy boundaries to your discussion. Use healthy time-limits. Violence is out of bounds. Immediately leave the room and/or the house if your partner gets violent. The saying is "Hurt me once, your mistake. Hurt me twice, my mistake." Violence is a reason to end the relationship.

Fathers and Fathering

Men have louder voices, stronger upper bodies, more muscles, greater height, larger size, and more testosterone than women. Men are often unconsciously socialized to violence through team sports and media. Their physicality is naturally more aggressive than a woman's. Often, men don't register the many powers they have—especially when seen through a woman's eyes.

Women can be easily frightened by a man's physical power. Men must learn to adjust their power, so it is respectful to a woman's vulnerability and not overpowering her.

Physical abuse is when you raise your voice, become violent, or throw things. A woman sees the object that is thrown as herself. Women's nervous systems overload more easily than men's. When a man raises his voice to a woman, it is damaging to her. By contrast, another man may not be negatively affected.

Emotional abuse is when you shame, disrespect, insult, or manipulate your partner's feelings, beliefs, or spiritual practice.

Any kind of abuse—whether it is physical, emotional, mental, spiritual, financial, or sexual—involves a tyrant and a victim. Abuse comes with an imbalance of power, grandiosity, and lack of respect.

For healthy communication, stay on topic. Don't gunny-sack a long list of previously unresolved complaints. Stay present with one issue at a time. If you find yourself going into the past, pull your focus back to the current topic.

Say what you need and want. It works best to say what you ***do want*** rather than only saying what you don't want. Give your partner a path to success by stating exactly what you want and how she can deliver it.

For healthy communication, here are some **common traps to avoid**. They can flag the need for better skills:

- Name-calling.
- Insulting.
- Disrespect.
- Using the phrase: "You always ___" or "You never ___."
- Making "you" statements rather than saying "I." Rather than

saying "You did ___", practice saying "I feel..."
- Endlessly recalling the past without resolution.
- Gunny-sacking additional complaints.
- Blaming.
- Shoulding.
- Shaming.
- Guilting (guilt-inducing) your partner.
- Power imbalance.

In healthy arguing, you argue to resolution. No one blockades, avoids, hides, or withholds. Both parties tell the truth as gently as possible. It is only through truth-telling that resolution can be reached.

Take a break if tensions run too high. Plan to resume later. Go in the other room or leave the house. Physically exercise for a while until the energy clears.

Healthy communication means owning personal pain, rather than projecting it onto your partner. Making "I" statements is more successful than "You did..." accusations.

Healthy love is based on trust. In healthy love, no one controls or manipulates. The relationship is dynamic, open, and flowing. When healthy boundaries are crossed, the situation is honestly addressed. Everyone's power of "No" is honored. Partners confess when they are wrong. They ask for forgiveness, make amends, and change negative behavior.

ACTIVE LISTENING

When your partner speaks, it is important to listen with a soft heart and a full range of feelings. Open yourself to unify with your partner's journey, even though it's radically different from your own. Listen with empathy, as if your partner's pain were your own.

When your partner confronts you with negative emotions, use the **I'm on Your Side Technique**. Repeat exactly what you hear her say—as closely as you can.

Name and validate her experience. Honor and affirm her negative emotions as if you are walking in her shoes. Say, "No wonder you felt angry when I didn't come home until 1 AM. You were afraid and alone. It was disrespectful and selfish that I didn't call."

When your partner feels heard, respected, and understood, it's amazing how quickly arguments resolve. The comedian Rodney Dangerfield says "I don't get no respect!" All most of us want is a little respect—for what we feel, for what we need, and for who we are.

After your partner feels heard, you can both design a solution to the problem. The discussion moves back-and-forth between you, until both of you are satisfied. Active listening involves both hearing and speaking.

HEALTHY CONFRONTATION

When you have a difficult issue to confront, use **The Sandwich Technique: Good news. Bad news. Good news.**

Open your conversation with "Good news." You may use a compliment or an empathetic statement showing that you understand what your partner is feeling. Unify with your partner by naming and validating your partner's feelings and experience.

You might say, "When you stayed out so late last night with the boys, I know you deserve your time just for you. You work hard all week and you have a right to some fun."

After you've established a trust bridge, then mention your pain. You might say, "When you stayed out so late and didn't call, I felt anxious and worried. I wondered if you were safe. I really need you to call next time you are out late."

Now, close your "sandwich" with more good news. "The reason I worry about you is because I love you. I want you to be safe. I want us to enjoy a long, happy life together."

When healthy boundaries are violated, discuss your feelings. Don't endlessly delay facing a difficult issue. Clean up the mess. Delayed discussions have a way of compounding themselves. The negative feelings bring their friends!

Be sure to follow healthy confrontation with healthy resolution skills. Design a plan for the future to ensure that you both are happy. Perhaps, in the future if either spouse is gone past 11 PM, s/he calls. Find what is fair and what works for everyone.

Monitor yourself during confrontation. Make sure your anger is in check. Keep a soft heart. Relax your jaw. Breathe.

Openly discuss difficult subjects when everyone is fed, watered, rested, and undistracted. Turn the TV and phones off. Calendar time that is clear of interruptions.

IMPULSE CONTROL

The ability to control your external response is a sign of healthy adulthood. In healthy behavior, you don't just say whatever pops into your mind. You edit emotions for healthy communication.

If you listen to your partner with your heart, you are less likely to oppositionalize. Instant emotional reactivity must be packaged for external consumption. Anger is like TNT. It is volatile and destructive. It must be carefully managed.

Sometimes, a Time Out is necessary. If you are flooded with rage, move out of the room. Do physical exercise. Get out of the house until your head clears. Toxic dumping on your beloved is not appropriate.

Give yourself time and space to sort your internal feelings and beliefs. Discern where you differ from your partner. Re-engage your discussion later, after time to reflect in self-interview. Let cooler heads prevail.

Carefully monitor your interactions with your beloved. Notice when discussions step over the line into heated arguments. That is a potential danger zone signaling Time Out.

ENLISTMENT SKILLS

Once you gain self-knowledge through your self-interview skills, it is important to teach your beloved how to love you.

Don't assume s/he knows how to love you. What is obvious to you, may be obscure to your partner. The genders have radically different needs and desires. It is your job to enlist and teach your partner to love you in the way that you are designed to receive love.

And vice versa. Allow—even invite—your beloved to teach you how s/he needs to give and receive love.

Remember, men and women have vastly different nurturing styles. In his wonderful book *Men Are from Mars, Women Are from Venus*, Dr. John Gray says the genders speak different languages. It serves you to learn your partner's language so you can enlist her/m to help you.

In general, women need to hear: "I feel your pain." Men need to hear: "I see your view."

You must speak honestly of your needs and desires. It doesn't work to lie about what you feel. Nor does it work it try to fit your partner's ideal if it is dishonest for you. If a behavior is painful for you, it is probably not healthy giving.

To enlist your partner's support, it works best to say, "I need your help. Can you do _____ to help me?" It sounds like a minor difference, but if you say, "You need to _____", your partner can take offense, feel criticized, and become defensive.

Expressing your need for help is less controlling. It moves the discussion from power-plays to love. Your partner feels empowered by helping you.

CONFLICT-RESOLUTION SKILLS

Healthy communication and confrontation are followed by resolution. Definite action is taken to change and improve the situation. Clear agreements are made so the pain is not re-created in the future.

One sign of adulthood is that the healthy adult can give his word and keep it.

There are five ways to resolve an issue:

1. We do it your way.
2. We do it my way.

3. We do it your way, followed by my way.
4. Vice versa.
5. Or, we compromise.

The healthiest couples vary their resolution style, so the power flows between the two partners and doesn't get stuck, burdening one person repeatedly. The leadership role goes back and forth between spouses.

The epitome of dysfunctionality is the couple that has the same argument repeatedly, for years—or the couple that never argues. In times of conflict, when polarization is all you can see, remember: *There is always a third way!* Take a deep breath and let go!

Healthy confrontation and resolution skills identify a healthy marriage. When you are with a happily married couple, you get the sense that they can confront each other respectfully and find peaceful resolution. There is a sense of fairness and balance rather than control and violence. There is even humor. Neither partner takes himself too seriously.

The Hebrew tradition says that good loving actually attracts a love angel to the couple. The moment you open the door to where a loving couple lives, you can feel the presence of God in the Shekinah Angel, who resides inside the home. You can learn more on the American Angel Tradition from my other books and through Gateway University at www.GatewayUniversity.org.

Healthy conflict resolution requires humility and ownership. Partners say, "I'm sorry. I was wrong for the pain I caused. Please forgive me. You deserve better. How can I make it up to you? Our love is the greatest treasure of my life. I never should have been so unkind."

Healthy love means knowing how to say, "I'm sorry." Like praise, apology is best spoken, not implied.

The phrase "Please forgive me" goes a long way. It is very important.

When your partner is asking for forgiveness, give him a path to power to make amends. Decide what you need in order to restore trust. Then, enlist your partner to help you.

HEALTHY FAMILY

HEALTHY FAMILY CHARACTERISTICS

In order to see if your original family was healthy and to build a healthy family yourself, here are some additional characteristics of healthy marriage and family.

- Each family member **feels safe**. **No one feels erased**, unseen, wasted, or unvalued. As the poet said, "I held out my heart. You knew how to care for it, gently." Each person's experience is **respected and honored**. Family members are free to speak their minds, even if controversial, knowing they will be heard and seriously considered.

- It is safe to share and **discuss difficult emotions openly**. All family members **have a right to their true emotions**. No one needs to hide to feel safe. **No one has to pretend** they are strong, perfect, invisible, or not suffering. A full range of healthy emotions are named and validated.

- **Opinions vary** within the family. Members openly express separate opinions, emotions, and viewpoints. There are **many different ways to see** and do things. **There is no single, one right way**. Healthy families are **open, curious, and non-judgmental**—without being self-righteous or dogmatic.

- **Rules are not rigid, impossible, or tyrannical.** They can be updated as circumstances change. Rules are humane, reasonable, fair, and heart-centered. No one person has all the power. **Power is shared.** Over time, power and the leadership role move and are fluid. They are expressed through every member of the family. Energy flows among the members. **Family dynamics are flexible**, alive, and, open. They are not frozen or calcified.

- Members feel **connected, not isolated**. There is a sense of team identity and support. No one is demeaned or insulted.

- **No one is toxically shamed** because s/he has a negative emotion or a sexual urge. It is safe to have a full palette of emotions and desires, including healthy, connected, contained shadow emotions: anger, sadness, and fear.

- **Love is not abstract, theoretical, or philosophical. It is demonstrated and experienced**. Shakespeare said, "Love is not love that does not demonstrate." Love must be manifested and expressed. Family members do sweet, thoughtful, loving things for each other. Love is made!

- **Family members have relationship healthy skills** to resolve difficulties. These skills include: healthy boundaries, entitlement, self-interview, objective naming skills, truth-telling, healthy communication, active-listening, impulse control, healthy confrontation, enlistment, and conflict resolution.

- **Problems are handled openly, fairly, lovingly, and with wisdom.** Negative behavior is confronted, owned, and resolved.

- **Family members know the limits** of what is healthy behavior. They ask for forgiveness when they over-step healthy boundaries. They make amends and fix what they have broken.

- Through **resolution skills**, negative experiences are resolved in a timely manner. Humble apology and reparation are made if needed. And, the family moves on.

- In a healthy family, it is **safe to be vulnerable and to make**

mistakes. Members know mistakes will be dealt with fairly, with reparation, redemption, and even humor. Each member has the ability to own her/s mistake, to humbly ask forgiveness, to ask "How can I make it right?" and to make tangible changes.

When interviewed regarding her marriage to movie director Mike Nichols, journalist Diane Sawyer replied, "I wish someone had told me how great marriage could be! Mike's love for truth is so great and his integrity is so high, he makes it safe for me to say anything. There's no way I can make a mistake. He redeems everything I say with wisdom and humor."

In a healthy families, everyone gets their needs met. Each member has self-interview skills to know what s/he thinks, feels, hears, sees, desires, and dislikes. Each partner has communication skills to tell the truth about what s/he wants, in a way that is honest and not polarizing.

The partners know how to enlist each other to satisfy their needs. One love expert says, "You must be honest to feed yourself as well as your lover, so no one goes hungry." The unspoken rule is: We will work together to get everyone's needs met.

Problems get resolved. Outside help is enlisted if needed.

In a healthy family, there are few, if any, secrets. Some marriage experts say, "A family is as sick as its secrets." Total trust, sharing, and openness characterize healthy relationship. Hiding blocks true intimacy.

There are no power plays or rigid control issues. There are no master/slave polarizations. There is no tyrant/victim dynamic. No one is a martyr in the name of love. There is fair and equal work distribution. No one is held hostage.

In healthy relationships, there is a sense of team. Pioneering family psychologist, John Bradshaw's picture of the ideal marriage shows each partner playing a different instrument. Together they make beautiful music.

Team spirit and bonding originate from genuine, lived-love and the joy of shared experience. Family members genuinely enjoy and appreciate each other. There is a sense of humor and fun.

Recreational outings are planned, savored, and joyously anticipated.

Shared memories are valued as life's precious gifts. They are spoken of for years to come. Precious memories and family history are created together.

DYSFUNCTIONAL FAMILY CHARACTERISTICS

Here is the research identifying characteristics of dysfunctional marriage and family. Examine and notice the differences between the two lists. Identify your own childhood and parenting experiences.

- Dysfunctional families are **not safe. It is not safe to tell the truth** about what you see, feel, hear, know, perceive, desire, and dislike. Due to **toxic shaming**, no one dares to have an open and honest discussion.

- There are **no healthy coping skills** to handle emotions, desires, and conflict. Children are taught **not to value their emotions**. Emotions are not honestly named or valued. Everyone learns to **self-erase. You become invisible**, even to yourself.

- It may only be safe to **live from the waist up**. Perhaps, this is why there is a national epidemic of obesity. We stuff-down emotions with food. Without coping skills, it is unsafe to communicate about the lower three chakras including: survival, money, sex, and power. It's not permissible to be powerful or sexual. It's as if the human anatomy doesn't include genitalia.

- In some families, it may only be safe to **live from the neck up**. Intellectual achievement may be over-valued, while the rest of your experience is non-verbally shamed and judged unworthy. Mentalizing may be an escape from emotions and the messier issues of life.

- There is an unspoken **No-Talk Rule**, with severe limits regarding what is "improper" or "unacceptable." There are taboo subjects. **No one talks** about sex, money, power, or survival issues.

- **There are family secrets.**

- Only **one person has the power.** Power is not shared. There is a rigid family hierarchy. There is a **tyrant/martyr,** perpetrator/victim **dynamic** in the family. **Control and engulfment issues** abound. **Enmeshment and walling-off** demonstrate unhealthy boundaries among family members.

- Unhealthy families are **closed, dogmatic, and self-righteous.** There is only **one right way.** There is a sense of **oppression and heaviness.** Life is lived as a jail-sentence. Common scripts include: "Life is hard." "How I suffer." "Don't expect much."

- In dysfunctional families, false humility, self-sacrifice, false-giving, codependence, external performance, outer-oriented behavior, victimization, and **self-erasure may be rewarded as "spiritual." Pity-power** may be wielded in a desperate attempt to connect and to break the hypnotic trance of invisibility. There is often competition for pity-power.

- Unhealthy families are **rigid**. Energy and the leadership role do not flow among the members. Members feel **isolated and alone.** Members learn **self-erasure, denial, numbness, and invisibility** in order to survive.

- **They live like hostages on the frontlines of a warzone.** Studies done on survivors of dysfunctional families show the child's nervous system is comparable to soldiers on the frontlines of war. Survivors often suffer Post Traumatic Stress Disorder (PTSD).

- **No one communicates openly** with honest naming of feelings and vulnerability. It's not safe to be open and vulnerable. **Silence perpetuates** the hypnotic trance of the **family lie**. No one speaks up for justice and healthy behavior because members are ignorant of what is healthy. **No one knows what healthy behavior is!**

- **Humor may be caustic**, sadistic, bitter, or sarcastic. Jokes may be toxic—at someone else's expense. Family members

- are **targeted, scapegoated, or viciously insulted**—sometimes under the guise of humor.
- Pets can be abused to demonstrate dysfunctional or frustrated power.
- **Problems don't get resolved**. The family may have the same fight for years.
- Dysfunctional families come from the **principle of scarcity**. There is never enough love, time, skills, caring, energy, information, sharing, support, or attention. No one gets enough.
- **Because there is never enough**, family **members compete against each other** for what little there is. **Sibling rivalry** can be covert, virulent, toxic, and destructive.
- **Children may act-out** their frustration, anger, and unfulfilled needs destructively. Drug addiction, running-away, crisis addiction, lawlessness, promiscuity, sexual risks, teen pregnancies can be children's **self-destructive attempts to penetrate the family lie.**
- Instead of enjoying life together, members are reduced to **survival behaviors**.
- They don't share pleasant **daily rituals**. They often do not share meals together. They don't come together to exchange the good news/bad news of the day. They don't discuss their **daily victories and defeats.**
- Unhealthy families **don't laugh and have fun** together. There is no shared experience to look forward to. Unhealthy families **don't create treasured times together**.

Notice the glaring differences between healthy and toxic families. Where does your experience fall?

In healthy relationship, there is often a gardener and a rose. The best marriages are when each partner can play either role. Partners can switch back and forth. Sometimes, one gets the spot-light. Sometimes, the other is the center of attention.

In unhealthy families, there is no flow. Members are stiff, as if they've memorized their lines. They are not relaxed and natural with each other. They are on-guard like Cinderella's back-stabbing stepsisters. However, rather than stuffing their feet into too-small shoes, unhealthy family members cram their identities into rigid family rules that don't fit.

In healthy marriage and family, you can be yourself—warts and all. You actually feel more like yourself, when someone truly loves you. You don't worry about being criticized. You feel safe.

You say to your beloved, "Around you, I become who I want to be." You are relaxed and comfortable being yourself. In a destructive relationship, you have no clear sense of yourself.

If you want to know if you love someone, ask "Do I respect them?" And conversely, "Do I feel respected when I am with them?" Respect is the core of healthy love. You don't feel wasted or invisible with your beloved. Instead, you feel seen, valued, and empowered—the best version of yourself.

Healthy families speak to each other about their love, daily. They practice praise, routinely preening each other's feathers. Praise is spoken specifically and directly—not implied.

Healthy families have fun. They laugh together.

HEALTHY ADULTHOOD

Children learn respect for the law in families. Without respect for the law, children remain frozen in arrested development. Healthy laws are the foundation of civilization. When our families are at risk, so is our civilization.

Without respect for limits, humans become grandiose and shameless. They don't have access to healthy shame. *The function of healthy shame is to alert the conscience of a boundary infraction.*

Without healthy shame, there is a vacuum inside—where God belongs. The child might fill this gap with grandiosity, by playing God. Or, he may become polarized, bouncing between grandiosity and self-loathing. Neither extreme fills the hole in the soul.

Healthy shame signals that you have over-stepped the limits of your legitimate entitlement. You have disrespected boundaries—yours, another person's, or God's.

> **The difference between a child and an adult is that the adult respects the law.**
>
> **The laws of life define its limits.**
>
> **A healthy adult respects the limits—both of life and of love.**
>
> **With maturity, we accept life on life's terms, rather than our own.**

PETER-PAN-VILLE

Many adult-children are frozen in Peter Pan-ville, living in arrested development. Limited by selfish self-indulgence, Peter Pans have no adult accountability. Having survived dysfunctional families, they never saw a healthy adult. They were raised by adult-children.

There was no adult in charge of their childhood home. As children, they had **no models, no methods, no maps, and no mentors** for healthy adulthood. No wonder they choose to rebel and remain children as adults!

The abused child thinks, "I don't want to grow up and become like mom/dad! Mom/dad are all about suffering and dishonesty; tyranny and martyrdom. If that's what being an adult is, I refuse to do it!"

Peter Pans often are locked in the arrested development of the two-year old. They can be narcissistic, grandiose, egotistical, and self-centered. Refusing to respect adult limits, they may act-out aggression, become addicts, or break the law. They may have anger-management issues.

People who choose to remain as adult-children often witnessed terrible injustice as children. If your internal "Brat" is sitting on the throne running your Inner Kingdom, you may have childhood trauma to resolve.

With healthy adulthood, we respect that life and love have limits. We work to develop healthy boundaries, entitlement, communication, enlistment, and conflict resolution skills.

CODEPENDENCY

In addition to the arrested development of Peter Pan, there are many unhealthy family models of false-loving and false-giving. The codependent idea of unconditional love has also caused a lot of heart-ache and simply doesn't work.

Codependency is giving to get. It is manipulation rooted in the giver's unworthiness. Her only way of achieving value is through self-sacrifice. However, there is a huge difference between self-abnegation and selfless service. She falsely believes that her only value is in giving.

The codependent is unaware of her legitimate needs, desires, likes, dislikes, and entitlement. No one taught her how to do honest self-interview and to speak of her needs, her desires, her feelings, her thoughts, her beliefs. Over time, she self-erases.

Into the vacuum of self-erasure, she places an idealized view of "the other." Idealization helps her to survive, giving her a false sense of control. Idealization is disowned power because no one ever taught you how to love yourself.

The codependent manipulates others through her "good girl" giving. Her false model of love was learned in childhood. Her false-belief is that love requires martyrdom, suffering, and pain. "If it doesn't hurt, it's not love" is one of her unconscious scripts. The codependent gives from an empty cup.

She is muddled in masochistic, passive-aggressive confusion.

Both Peter Pan and the codependent are often survivors of dysfunctional families. Survivors have amazing resilience, loyalty, and perseverance. They are very strong, heroic people. Otherwise, they would not have survived the terrible injustices they suffered. One heroic survivor said, "I never would have loved so well if I had not been so broken."

HEALTHY LOVE

By contrast to dysfunctional relationship, a healthy marriage is organic, dynamic, messy—always moving and growing. A counselee once commented on how her marriage had reached a new level of fulfillment. "Now, if it would just stay still!"

However, life goes in cycles—always guaranteed to change, always generating new forms. Change itself is a sign of aliveness. In relationships, "still" can mean "dead". A healthy relationship is always changing. There are cycles of reward and victory.

The healthy adult develops skills to weather all cycles, both feast and famine.

CHILD ABUSE

SERVING THE CHILD

If you grew up in a dysfunctional family, the following information will help you in parenting your own child—both your inner child and your outer child. Some of the information may surprise you.

1. **The parent's job is to serve the child.** Unhealthy parenting is when the child serves the parent.

2. **The parent's job is to facilitate the child's healthy self-construction.** This is a time/labor intensive job. Without a healthy sense of self the child has difficulty facing adult life, relating to other people, pair-bonding, working, and trusting God.

3. **The parent's job is to name and to validate the child's experience.**

ABANDONMENT AND NEGLECT

If the parent tries to get his needs met through the child, no one serves the child. The child quickly learns self-abandonment, a lack of entitlement, and unhealthy boundaries. Unhealthy parenting is when the child serves the parent. Children need a safe, strong, reliable, authority figure who centers around them to guide their development.

Children are not little adults. Their brains are impressionable and easily programmed. Brain studies on children compare them to an adult in a hypnotic trance. Children are easily "hypnotized" to copy dysfunctional parental models when they raise their own children.

Abandonment and neglect define child abuse. In today's world, there are many forms of abandonment and neglect—including the parent's survival distraction to earn a living; parental absorption with the dating game; not enough daily parental quality-time with each child; addiction; and not providing adequate sex education for the child.

Many parents experience their children as burdens—financially, time-wise, and energetically. This psychic message is broadcast to the sensitive child, defining her self-worth as valueless.

Some parents experience their children as extensions of themselves, rather than as separate individuals. The parent may think of the child as an appendage—much like a fashion-accessory. The child exists to validate the parent, demonstrating his adult status and societal standing.

The child's proving the parent's self-worth is the reverse of healthy parenting. The child feels erased, unworthy, and de-valued. No one is serving the child's needs.

PARENTAL BUDDYING

Intrusive parenting across healthy boundaries is a popular form of child abuse. When the unhealthy parent treats the child as his best friend, there is inappropriate cross-generational bonding. If the parent is cross-gender, this "confiding in a friend" can be a form of emotional incest.

In parental buddying, the unformed child is expected to perform as an adult, to act as the parent's friend. However, the child is not an adult. The parent's projection of equality stresses the child's nervous system. Unprepared to meet this unfair expectation, the child feels burdened and overwhelmed—even engulfed—by the parent's neediness.

The child's need for a loving authority figure goes unmet. Intrusive parenting serves the parent's need for approval, attention, control, and conversation. Rather than serving the child's self-development and healthy boundaries, buddying serves parental neediness. It is the reverse of healthy parenting.

Without healthy boundaries, the child is protecting the parent at a time when the child needs protection himself. This unbalanced relationship damages the child, robbing his childhood.

The dysfunctional behavior of parental buddying reflects a vacuum in the parent's life. Instead of leaching energy from his child, the parent needs to create a social life with same-age friends.

LEARNED SELF-ABANDONMENT

By protecting the parent, the child learns self-abandonment rather than healthy self-construction. Serving parental neediness, the child has no healthy entitlement or healthy boundaries. Rescuing the parent, the child adopts outer-oriented behavior, rather than healthy, internal self-care.

Somewhere deep inside, the child feels something is off, but he blames himself. The child assumes, "Daddy is the adult. He must know best. I must be wrong." The child erases himself.

ENMESHMENT

When the child rescues the parent, the child sacrifices his own selfhood. He merges with his parent's identity. This enmeshment replaces healthy self inside the child. The child is bereft, without independent identity.

If your parents never taught you how to develop a separate self, you never learned basic self-interview skills: What do I feel? What do I want? What do I need? What do I think?

You become numb inside, dismembered from your true self. Your decisions are externalized, based on parental approval rather than on your true desire. You live your parent's life better than your own.

As the parent's caretaker, the abused child reverses normal, healthy behavior. This unhealthy reversal of internal wiring affects the child's ability to form healthy relationships as an adult.

REVERSED-WIRING

When a child grows up in a dysfunctional family, she learns that unhealthy behavior is the norm. Her nervous system reverses healthy behavior. With reversed-wiring, as an adult when she goes toward sick behavior, it feels normal and familiar from childhood. It feels like love, like home.

When she is exposed to healthy behavior, it feels foreign, even suspicious and unsafe. She experiences healthy love as a trap. She may not be able to breathe. In a healthy relationship, she feels lost and confused

Sadly, when she goes toward dysfunctional love, it is comfortable and familiar. She experiences toxic love as just right. With reversed wiring because of childhood trauma, when she goes toward death, it feels like life. When she goes toward life, it feels like death.

Child abuse undermines a child's healthy survival instincts. In the reversed-wiring of child abuse, pain is encoded as life-giving love. Healthy love is coded as death. The adult-child literally experiences life as death; and death as life. The reversed-wiring of child abuse is insidious, subliminal, and destructive.

> **There is a tragic reversal of internal wiring caused by child abuse.**
>
> **Reversed-wiring makes it difficult for the adult to pair-bond, find happiness, make healthy choices, or develop healthy selfhood.**

If this weren't bad enough, without healthy selfhood, the adult cannot access a healthy God. Parental abuse from childhood is projected onto the ultimate authority figure, God. The adult-child invents a deranged God. His God may be an overly punishing God with revenge wars, a self-indulgent God with obesity epidemics, or an entirely absent God with atheism.

DAMAGED CHOICE MECHANISM

The reversed wiring of child abuse undermines healthy instincts and constructive choices. An abused child doesn't know what she feels, what she thinks, or what she desires. No one has taught her to name her emotions, to do self-interview, or to construct healthy selfhood.

Access to this vital self-knowledge is twisted and frozen in internal fear, chaotic impressions, and toxic shame-binds. The adult-child literally does not know what normal is. She doesn't have a clue regarding healthy choices. She has a damaged choice mechanism.

Numbed by the hypnotic trance of an abusive childhood, the adult-child lacks basic, healthy entitlement and healthy boundaries. How can she properly defend herself? She is like a zombie, sleep-walking through life, paralyzed by lack of self-awareness. If she doesn't know how she feels, what she thinks, or what she desires, how can she make healthy choices?

The abuse survivor lives with a damaged choice mechanism. She can be flooded and overwhelmed by a simple shopping trip where she must choose between two pairs of shoes!

VACUUM OF SELFHOOD

Without healthy selfhood, a vacuum exists inside the child. In an effort to fill the emptiness, the child overly identifies with her abuser. To fill the hole of selfhood, she substitutes her abuser's identity.

The child never realizes she has lost her authentic selfhood. If you don't know something exists—such as selfhood—how would you know you lost it?!

Without access to healthy selfhood, the child can never psychologically separate from mommy/daddy. Parents continue to run the show inside her. Tragically, she can never individuate. She remains in limbo, unconsciously bound to parents, trapped inside a psychological trance induced in childhood.

The abused child has no healthy parental anchor. The systematic destruction of healthy selfhood completely disorients the bereft child.

TRAUMA BINDS

Toxic parenting traumatizes the tiny child. It creates trauma-binds between the child and her abuser. These unnatural binds are powerful since the child is in a hypnotic state, vulnerable, and susceptible to parental programming.

Studies show that the damage done to an abused child's nervous system is comparable to that suffered by soldiers on the frontlines of war. Literally, the abused child normalizes "life as war." The residue of PTSD in our damaged children masquerades in a vast assortment of adult, mental illnesses.

Note from a mystic: Beyond this incarnation, the traumatic memory can take lifetimes to unravel and to detoxify. The pattern of trauma can reoccur across lifetimes!

Trauma opens the child's aura and deepens her hypnotic trance—beyond reach of the conscious mind. The child becomes melded into the parent's identity—as if the two people were one.

Trauma-binds affect both boys and girls. These unconscious pain-binds make it difficult for the child to separate or to individuate from mom/dad in normal, healthy, adult individuation.

The child habituates to adrenalin, panic, hyper-vigilance, and stressful living. These extremes become normalized.

BLOCKED INDIVIDUATION

With healthy maturation, the child separates from parents to develop her own identity. That's why God created adolescent rebellion; so the child can individuate from mommy/daddy! Without healthy adolescent rebellion, the child can remain bound to the parent's identity, locked in arrested development.

If you are enmeshed with mom/dad through trauma-binds, you can't access your own, separate identity. Without realizing it, you have a vacuum of self inside. Into that vacuum, you substitute your parents' identity. You misconstrue their identity, assuming it is your own.

You are unconsciously submerged in parental scripts, beliefs, values, and identities. You experience your parents as yourself.

Enmeshment creates the child in psychological bondage to the parents. She is invisibly bound and gagged—isolated from her independence and adulthood. She has not properly individuated.

If you experienced child abuse, without knowing it, you may be living in the limbo of arrested development—much like a psychological prisoner. You may be paralyzed, unable to access healthy selfhood. If you have not separated from your parents, you may be living your parent's dream instead of your own. You may not be able to individuate into your authentic adulthood.

You may be a *puer eternis*, an eternal child, living as an adult-child.

CHILD ABUSE TALLY

The preceding chapter shows the devastation and dereliction of unhealthy parenting. Some of the damage done to the child includes:

> Learned self-abandonment, enmeshment, reversed-wiring, damaged choice-mechanism, vacuum of selfhood, trauma-binds, blocked individuation, arrested development, action derangement, disabled will, lack of healthy selfhood, no healthy boundaries, no healthy entitlement, no objective naming skills for emotions, no self-interview skills, no healthy communication skills, lack of empathy, lack of confrontation skills, lack of impulse control, lack of enlistment skills, lack of conflict resolution skills, unresolved trauma, stress, PTSD, toxic shaming, and a twisted internal voice that's either martyring or tyrannical.

The terrible tally of destruction done to the child makes it difficult for her to pair-bond, to work, to trust other people, to trust life, or to trust God. Without a healthy sense of self, the child has difficulty facing adult life. Functioning without self-destruction or attacking others can be challenging. Earning a living can feel like climbing Mt. Everest. Creating a basic, happy life can be allusive.

The adult-child's internal self-talk is often chaotic, twisted, paranoid, anxious, or negative. The inner voice often unconsciously involves self-shredding and decimation. The survivor may experience life as an isolation or a torture chamber. Escaping into drugs, alcohol, promiscuity, or thrill-seeking can be a misplaced attempt to stop the pain.

THE ADULT-CHILD IN LEADERSHIP

The abundance of dysfunctional families is a primary reason you see so many adult-children in the culture—even running government, Wall Street, media, and high positions of global power. The profligate self-indulgence of many nations demonstrates avoidance of healthy, adult limits.

Adults have limits. Children do not. Setting limits is a basic, boundary skill of healthy selfhood taught in childhood by healthy parenting.

However, rather than adult compromise, too often governments squabble like children—even throwing chairs and punches! There is no adult in charge! Many governments and leaders across the world are adult-children, locked in immature behavior. They demonstrate arrested development from dysfunctional parenting.

Families are where children learn morality, how to obey rules, and respect for the law. Without limits, behavior is shameless. Without healthy families, civilization is at risk. Healthy parenting is essential to our survival—both personally and globally.

HEALTHY PARENTING

THE PARENT'S JOB

A healthy parent does the following:

1. **The parent's job is to serve the child.** Unhealthy parenting is when the child serves the parent. We have seen this dysfunctional parenting in the preceding chapter on *Child Abuse.*
2. **The parent's job is to facilitate the child's healthy self-construction.** In the preceding chapter on *Healthy Marriage,* we have learned healthy self-construction and relationship skills.
3. **The parent's job is to name and to validate the child's experience.** The following chapter provides healthy skills to name and validate your child's emotions and experience.

HEALTHY SELF-CONSTRUCTION

The parent must teach the child healthy selfhood. Healthy selfhood is not innate. Without civilization, children can be unruly animals. Lacking a healthy sense of self, the child can't face adult life properly. He may remain in arrested development and become an adult-child.

The following skills are essential for healthy self-construction and healthy adulthood. Without healthy selfhood, how can you have a healthy relationship with anyone else? If you are numb regarding your emotions, you are numb to yourself. Your relationship to your self—and even to God—is tragically robbed.

Without healthy selfhood, the abused child grows up carrying an unconscious script that everyone else knows something important, while he is left-out. He thinks, "They received the Training Program and the Manual, but I didn't." He feels alienated, like an outsider to life.

Sadly, he is correct. He never received his basic entitlement, healthy selfhood.

He may turn inward, blaming himself in endless shame and self-persecution. Or, he may project outward, masquerading in grandiosity as a cover for powerlessness.

---

11 HEALTHY SELF-CONSTRUCTION SKILLS

1. **Boundaries**
2. **Entitlement**
3. **Self-Interview**
4. **Objectively Naming Emotions**
5. **Truth-Telling**
6. **Communication**
7. **Active Listening with Empathy**
8. **Confrontation**
9. **Impulse Control**
10. **Enlistment**
11. **Conflict Resolution**

See the previous chapters on *Healthy Marriage* and *Child Abuse* for a detailed description of the above skills—**except #4 Objectively Naming Emotions**. *Healthy Marriage* describes "10 Skills for Healthy Self and Relationship." The current chapter on *Healthy Parenting* drills deeper, emphasizing the importance of naming emotions for healthy self-development.

NAMING EMOTIONS

A healthy parent names and validates the child's emotions and experience—even when it is negative or painful. Rather than avoiding the subject, the parent opens the conversation about difficult emotions. The parent draws out the child's story, listening carefully to the child's view.

Healthy parents listen with the heart. They listen as if the child's journey were their own. They reflect the child's experience back to him—naming and valuing each emotion in his story.

By naming and valuing emotions, the child discerns his internal and external worlds, making sense of them. He gains a sense of control. Rather than jumbled chaos, named emotions become manageable. The child feels legitimatized and begins to discover fairness. He feels less alone, knowing that his parents have traveled the same journey as his own.

Rather than toxically shaming the child for shadow emotions— anger, sadness, and fear—the healthy parent considers them legitimate. The parent might say: "I hear that you are angry because Madison stole your book. I don't blame you. I would be angry too. That book belonged to you. He had no right to take it."

Emotions don't lie. They are like the weather. Emotions just are.

What you do with emotions can either be healthy or unhealthy. It is important to own and to resolve shadow emotions through honest self-interview and clear naming. First, the toxic emotion must be acknowledged.

When healthy emotional training and self-construction are lacking, the child grows to adulthood not knowing what "normal" is. The adult-child can either over-express or under-express emotions, inappropriately.

NAMING WITHOUT TOXIC SHAME

- Naming is clear perceiving and honest reporting. Naming is objective, empty, and non-judgmental. Rather than a power game, there is no ego involved. There is no moralizing or self-righteousness.

- Naming the child's journey is not about the parent's frustration. Rather, naming identifies the child's behavior and emotions.

- The child's behavior and emotions are not who he is. Just as clouds pass over the sky, emotional weather changes. By contrast, your essence doesn't change.

- You have power to change your behavior and emotions. However, you don't have power to change your intrinsic design. Your essence is the way God made you.

- Contrasted with naming emotions, toxic shaming is judgmental. It is separative, hierarchical consciousness. It is a power game serving the parent's ego. Discharging the parent's emotional frustration, toxic shame serves the parent rather than the child.

- Toxic shame trauma-binds the bad behavior and negative emotions to the child's intrinsic identity.

- Toxic shame insults the child's basic design, which is the way God made him. Your essence is not changeable. It is like your skin color. Toxic shame condemns your value and self-worth. It removes your right to exist.

- Toxic shaming leaves the child powerless to change.

- Behavior is an epiphenomenon, an external layer over your essence. You have power to change your behavior and emotions. By contrast, you cannot change your essence.

Naming your child's emotions and experience without toxic shaming teaches him to delineate his self-worth from his behavior. He separates his emotions from his identity.

Once separated, he has leverage to change his behavior. He has power over his emotions. Naming his journey gives him a path to power. You empower your child.

On the other hand, toxic shame attacks the child's unchangeable, intrinsic design—the way God made him. Insulting God's design deeply and profoundly decimates the child's value. Expecting a turtle to be a race horse erases the turtle's gift for self-protection and survival. Toxic shame destroys your child's dignity and self-worth.

In addition, judging God's design as inferior is grandiose. The judge sets himself above God. Toxic shaming is godless behavior.

Naming is about your external behavior and emotions. Simple naming objectively addresses a situation that you have power to change. However, insulting your child's design through toxic shame removes his path to power and leaves him powerless.

TOXIC VS. HEALTHY SHAME

Everything on earth has duality. Everything has a front and a back; a beginning and an ending; good and bad aspects. Similarly, there is both healthy and unhealthy shame.

The purpose of healthy shame is to set healthy limits. For example, wearing your clothes in public sets a healthy limit or law for the culture as a whole.

Naming and setting healthy limits for a child teaches him conscience. It teaches respect for the law. Healthy limits define the healthy boundaries of civilization and the self. Without laws, there is chaos and arrested development. Evolution and maturation can't take place.

Simple naming without blaming or judgment teaches the child healthy shame. The child learns the acceptable limits of life. Through a careful analysis of each situation, the parent leads the child to see what works in life. The child learns to assess enduring life values rather than to indulge instant gratification.

For example, the parent might say "When you exploded at your teacher in class, what did you feel?" "What did your angry expression give you?"

The child might reply, "Relief. Satisfaction. Power. Justice." The parent and child might explore the relative values and duration of each victory, as well as its subsequent repercussions. How long did the victory feelings last? What was momentary relief? What price did you pay for short-term satisfaction? What might enduring relief look like? How did the teacher feel? How did the class feel? How do you want others to see you?

Depending upon the age of the child, the parent and child might discuss impulse control, which is the privilege of growing-up and carrying increased powers. Everything in life comes with a price. Mature behavior requires increased skills. Managing emotions in a healthy way is part of adult life.

Healthy shame teaches the child that we all are human. We are not God. Everyone is broken in some way. That is part of the human experience. Duality comes with your birth certificate. No human is perfect. We all are learning.

Through healthy shame, the child learns not to judge others. They are simply learning through painful, negative experiences—just as he does.

Without healthy shame, the child becomes grandiose, playing God. There is no room for God when a human occupies that throne. The child becomes godless—without conscience or healthy limits. Lawless behavior fosters criminals.

> **Healthy shame teaches humility.**
> **No one is perfect. To be human is to be limited.**
> **Only God is without limits.**
> **Behaving without healthy shame is playing god.**
> **It is grandiosity**.

By contrast to healthy shame, **toxic shame models the parent's godless, egotistical behavior to the child**. It is separative, insulting the child's very essence. If a mother screams at her son, "Do I have to come in there and wipe your ass?" she has offended the child's dignity and gender. She has crossed a personal boundary, decimating his self-respect and his right to exist.

She sends the message that he is the one person on earth that God abandoned. He is unworthy of loving or living. **Toxic shame is soul murder.**

Toxic parenting is tragically unhealthy. Although the mother's anger is temporarily relieved, she is teaching her son to love/hate her, women, God, life, and himself. She guarantees that future crises will ensue as his crippled selfhood unfolds.

A healthy parent gives the child a path to power by reinforcing the child's natural, inherent dignity. For example, the parent might say, "You are a strong and intelligent boy. I know you didn't mean to drop the ketchup bottle. I'll help you to clean it up." While they are both cleaning, the parent can recommend future behaviors that are not so risky in handling the ketchup; then, ask the child to choose which one feels comfortable.

HEALTHY SHADOW EMOTIONS

It's the parent's job to model and to teach the child healthy management of emotions. In healthy relationships, each person takes responsibility for her emotions. Each person names her emotions—both the light and shadow emotions.

It's important to speak of difficult emotions and to resolve them. If you are a survivor of a dysfunctional family, you may deny, avoid, or numb-out to negative emotions.

Begin by naming your child's emotions. Ask her "What are you feeling? Are you mad, sad, or afraid?" These are the basic shadow emotions. Emotions are valuable because they don't lie. They connect you with the truth of your being.

Shadow emotions—such as anger, fear, and sadness—have both healthy and unhealthy expressions. It is healthy to name and resolve negative emotions. It is unhealthy to repress, disown, project, or over-express them.

All shadow emotions signal the need for change. Ask: What is the uncomfortable emotion saying? What is it teaching you? What do you want that you don't currently have? What must change in your life? What does the negative emotion prevent you from experiencing or doing? What will replace the anger, sadness, or fear when it is gone?

Receive the gifts of wisdom and information from your shadow emotion. Listen to its script. Let it teach you. Negative emotions can help you to grow.

Healthy anger is a form of vitality, useful for survival. **Anger signals a boundary invasion**. It defines healthy limits. It alerts you to an entitlement issue. Anger lets you know something you value has been hurt, stolen, or damaged. It's like an alarm system telling you that someone has entered your house uninvited.

What you do with anger is important. Healthy anger must be contained within respectful boundaries, connected to specific events, expressed appropriately, and resolved in a timely manner.

It's healthy to feel anger when someone robs what is yours or abuses your personal power. You have a right to your healthy anger. Healthy anger is your ally.

By contrast, unhealthy anger is unresolved, disowned, disproportionate, uncontained, projected onto others, and disrespectful. It may be disconnected from reality and inappropriate to the situation. If you reverse-engineer unhealthy anger, it may originate in childhood trauma. Violence is never acceptable, in childhood or adulthood.

Through healthy anger, you affirm what is rightfully yours. You fight for justice. Anger helps you to repel negative invasion, injustice, or dishonesty.

Healthy anger guarantees that you don't enmesh with or wall-off from others. To maintain healthy boundaries, you must assert your power of "No!"

Healthy anger demonstrates your life-force. It focuses your strength to fight for survival or to defend justice.

When you are self-interviewing and naming your emotions—for your inner or your outer child—you will discover that resolving anger happens in layers. Under the opening layer of anger, there is a deeper layer of hurt. Perhaps, a false expectation, a hope, or a treasured belief that was damaged or lost. Once you discover the hurt, under that there is sadness and loss.

Patiently, sit and name your child's journey, each step of the way uncovering layer upon layer of emotions. Name and validate each emotion for the child. Teach your child to value the slow unfolding of the layers in God's mysterious teachings.

Under the layers of anger, hurt, loss, and sadness, you will find love. Your child loved and cherished something that was lost. Find the gift of wisdom that replaces the loss. What did you learn from the experience? How have you grown stronger? What have you discovered about yourself? How has your identity expanded?

As she answers each question, guide your child to open and to receive her new greatness. Value her new wisdom. Show her how courageous she is to face the anger and to find the wisdom gift.

Honor her for loving herself enough to grow. Say, "I'm proud of you for diving deeply inside and learning new skills." Praise your child's journey to adulthood. Teach her to value her wisdom treasures.

Pain is often the price of power and growth. We take wisdom from the wound. In transmuting negative energy to positive, always ask: What is the gift in the pain? Go toward the gift, rather than away from the pain. Treasure the gift as a jewel in your crown of wisdom.

The healthy function of sadness is to signal loss. Grief creates space for new life and new identity. Healthy sadness says goodbye to the past and opens the door to a new future. Grief provides the labor pains to birth your new identity.

To successfully negotiate loss, you must love God's wisdom more than what you have lost. Through loss, you surrender to God's will. Sacrifice is sacramental. It consecrates your life. Through loss, you ride deeper into God's embrace.

Find the wisdom gift in the pain. What are you learning? How are you growing? What new power are you gaining? What wisdom replaces the loss? How is your identity changing?

Some losses are irreplaceable at the human level. The gift in the exchange is expanded consciousness. As you learn a new emptiness, you embrace eternal Truth. Praise yourself for having the courage to value God's Truth beyond your own suffering.

Enlightenment is a grief experience. The *Bible* says, "The price of wisdom is grief." Making friends with the emptiness of grief teaches self-soothing and surrender.

Every child must learn that life has limits. **Grief often signals the limits of your control.** Grief helps us to process and to digest the limits of life. Learning that we have no control over some events teaches respect for a Higher Power.

To resolve grief, you must transcend events, trusting the Unknown—The Great Mystery—trusting a Higher Power. Transcending events is an irrational act. There is no motivation except God union and resolution of pain. Sometimes, you experience pain until you accept God's plan beyond your own.

The grieving process involves: denial, bargaining, anger, depression, and finally acceptance. Each person grieves differently, with a different timetable.

Healthy fear tells you to proceed with caution for safety. Fear shows a need for clarity, help, movement, change, or information. Who or what is safe? Where must I move for safety? What is right-action? Where is my power? Who can help me?

Fear signals a need for self-protection. The direction you are going is not safe. You may need to reach out for support or help. You may need more information or increased clarity. Call on friends for help.

Is the fear legitimate or imagined? Does it come from the past? Or is it fear of the future?

Sometimes the medicine for fear is as the Ram Dass book title says: *Be Here Now*. The solution may be as simple as "Breathe." Or, stay connected with your body. You may need grounding in the present moment instead of catastrophizing about an imagined future.

Fear can teach faith. Sometimes, you overcome disproportionate, unhealthy fear by trusting in your Higher Power. Are you false-godding from disease labels, money problems, other people, or worldly events? You can either have your fear or faith.

Fear may be saying, "Surrender. This problem is beyond your tiny, human means to solve. Let go and let God support you. God is in charge!" Plug-in to your Infinite Resource and Supply. Trust life's process.

SELF-SOOTHING

Healthy parents teach the child self-soothing skills as a path to the child's independence. Skills begin in toddler years when the child is given a favorite teddy bear or blanket to make sleeping alone safe. Parent's sing lullabies to usher the child into the sleep realms. Nightly rituals, such as reading a story and saying prayers, restore the child's confidence before sleep.

To teach self-soothing in teen years, it's important for parents to name the child's terrors; then, to validate each fear. Rather than taking the fear away, go into it with your child.

Enter the child's world and value her experience. For example, say, "No wonder you were terrified to make the speech in front of the class and that horrible boy. He cat-called you last week! He must be raised in a cave by savages! At your age, I would have been terrified." Unify with your child and name her emotions **using an "I'm-on-Your-Side Technique."**

Then, build a word-picture, visually imaging possible resolutions. **Make a movie in your mind.** Use yourself as a model, even if it's a hypothetical fantasy. For example, you might say, "When I had a similar experience in high school, as I gave my speech, I looked the savage right in the eye and visualized a Mickey Mouse hat with big, wiggly, black, mouse-ears on his head. I laughed inside! Ha! I took my power back. I was not going to allow him to steal it!"

The parent names and values the child's experience, thus validating the child. Then, the parent builds a bridge to power, modeling healthy behavior for the child.

The parent might continue by offering the classic, public speaking advice: "My friend had a similar experience with another caveman boy. My friend imagined the kid naked in the Arctic Circle in winter!" Laughter and exaggerated mind-pictures can break the emotional lock for a child, releasing her from Pain Prison and returning her to her power.

Self-soothing skills make it safe for the child to enter adulthood. Over time, the healthy parental voice internalizes. As a healthy adult, she invents her own self-soothing scripts. She has learned self-empowerment.

THE CHILD'S SOUL

Your love-energy deposits inside your child. As you lovingly guide her through naming and resolving complex emotions, she develops an internal gyroscope for centering. A comforting inner voice tells her, "You can face this problem just like you did with mom and dad." The child builds an internal track-record of success, like an energy bank of wisdom inside her.

Your inner voice of loving guidance aligns her with the vibration of her own soul. Your healthy parenting literally connects your child with her Divine Mother—her lifetime supply of love and wisdom. As she grows to maturity, she learns to rely on her soul for comfort, renewal, and wisdom. She lives a soul embodied life.

As an adult she has inner resources and supply. She can access healthy conscience. She is never alone with her soul to guide her.

Your divine power as a parent is to activate your child's soul. Any time you feel love as a parent, you embody your soul on earth. Your soul is your feeling of love. Your loving soul-vibration transfers to your child.

A sympathetic vibration activates inside her. She now has access to her own soul. You have installed her God connection.

Do you see the awesome, divine dispensation of parenting?! What a sacred opportunity parenting is! You are God's agent in your child's life. In addition, loving your child helps you to consciously acknowledge your own divine equipment.

DAD'S PSYCHOLOGICAL LEGACY

DAD'S MODEL

The strongest role model in a child's life is the same-gender parent. If a son enjoyed healthy fathering, the child may model his adulthood based on his father's example—including dad's values, rituals, and behaviors.

If, however, the child experienced toxic fathering, the adult may choose to become the opposite of dad. Or, the son can internalize toxic dad and repeat the toxic parenting, visiting the sins of the father "unto the thirteenth generation" as the *Bible* says.

If a boy sees his dad abuse his mother, the child intrinsically knows the behavior is unjust. However, the child is powerless to protect his mother. Unable to stand against injustice, he is split from his power and from his manhood. He is bereaved of his healthy male identity by his dad's toxic modeling. These internal splits make it difficult for the boy to find healthy adulthood.

Witnessing abuse abuses the child. It can turn the boy against his own gender internally, in subtle but devastating ways. It can turn him against himself in self-destructive behaviors, disorienting healthy selfhood.

If a daughter admired dad, she might choose a mate who resembles dad. If, however, she experienced toxic fathering, she might choose the opposite of dad for her final mate. However, she can suffer some toxic mates along the way.

Before conscious awakening, a woman's early choice in pair-bonding often is a partner who subconsciously embodies father-qualities that the woman is psychologically digesting.

Before conscious awakening, a woman's early choice in pair-bonding often is a partner who subconsciously embodies father-qualities that the woman is psychologically digesting.

Yes, folks, we digest each other throughout life! We digest the people and events of each day. Notice the ones that create indigestion. Some digestions may require decades to complete!

Child abuse is defined by abandonment, neglect, or inappropriate boundaries. If you routinely suffered any of these as a child—psychologically or physically, you may be a survivor of child-abuse. You may have experienced toxic dad.

TOXIC CHOICES

If the daughter experienced toxic fathering, she may replicate dad by choosing a toxic husband. Toxic love is all the child knows. As an adult, she unconsciously feels drawn to abusive partners—since that is her experience of love from childhood.

With toxic parenting, love and pain twist together and merge inside the child. These trauma-binds become normalized. The child assumes everyone lives as she does.

The survivor acclimates and numbs to pain. Not knowing what healthy looks like, she experiences pain as the way of daily life. Studies show that survivors have the highest pain threshold of any population.

Pleasure/pain circuits reverse in the abused child. Love is deeply associated with pain.

As an adult, her internal reversed-wiring drives her to unhealthy choices for a mate. When she goes toward painful, toxic love, it is familiar from childhood. She experiences abuse as love. Like a well-programmed robot, she unconsciously chooses toxic partners.

Toxic parenting has robbed her of authentic choice.

LOST IDENTITY

Toxic parenting creates trauma-binds in the child. Trauma-binds affect both boys and girls. In addition to damaged choice-mechanism, these unconscious trauma-binds make it difficult for the child to separate or to individuate from mom/dad in normal, healthy development.

If you are locked in trauma from the past, you may have difficulty seeing mom/dad objectively. Part of your identity is consumed by them. The trauma may bind you to them, so you never properly individuate.

You may choose a life-partner to please them rather than yourself.

ARRESTED DEVELOPMENT

The adult-child can remain a psychological baby throughout life. Healthy adult development is frozen, arrested in childhood. Rather than inhabit life fully—with access to a full-range of emotions, behaviors, and choices—the adult-child robotically moves through his days, haunted by unconscious, childhood ghosts. He is unable to progress through the developmental tasks of maturation.

> **The adult-child may unconsciously replicate the father's toxic behavior—either externally in the way he treats others; or internally in the way he treats himself, with toxic self-talk.**

Conversely, the son who experienced toxic fathering can model his manhood radically differently—even opposite—from dad's image. However, just because you oppositionalize against dad doesn't mean that you find your own identity. Dad is still driving your identity and your life.

Either extreme of replication or polarizing represents arrested development in the adult-child. The adult-child has not found himself as a uniquely separate individual.

The adult-child is basically an automaton, engineered by undigested, childhood trauma. Toxic dad continues to drive the adult-child's life, until he awakens from his childhood nightmare. Only by seeing the damage done by toxic dad can the son or daughter regain their lost power.

Consciously witnessing the negative, hypnotic programming of childhood, the adult-child can move forward into healthy, adult development. Such awakening is rigorous. It is usually achieved through deep psychological or spiritual work with a guide.

Without awakening, the adult remains a child.

BIRTH PLACEMENT

Birth placement also affects a son's choice of his manhood design. The youngest son in a large family may choose an older brother or an uncle as his primary male-model, depending upon the family dynamics.

ABSENT DAD

If dad is absent much of the time, the child might create a composite manhood-design. Sadly, sometimes the most intimate relationship a child has is with TV personifications of fatherhood. To design his manhood, the son may cobble together images from neighbors and the media.

If the girl experiences absentee dad, she also may create a composite manhood design. She may amalgamate images from neighbors and the media to design her ideal man.

Absentee dad is often interpreted psychologically by the child as:

- I am less valuable than dad's time elsewhere.
- Dad doesn't value me.
- I am unworthy.

- I am unlovable.
- I must be broken.
- I must have done something bad.
- I'll try to be good, so dad won't leave me.

These abandonment and neglect scripts can become internalized and determine the child's inner life as an adult.

DAD/ MOM INTERNALLY

Both boys and girls internalize their experience of mom/dad. The child digests the parental model to become his own unconscious psychology. The adult either imitates the parental model or polarizes from it.

If the child experienced toxic parenting, as an adult he may have a twisted internal male or female archetype. Unwinding the complexity of internalized mom and dad may require effort.

There may be trauma-binds to both parents that make it difficult for the adult-child to mature in a healthy manner. Crises may ensue.

DAD/MOM: ACTIVE AND RECEPTIVE PRINCIPLES

Father embodies the male principle of will, assertion, forward movement, dominion, power, and invulnerability. Mother embodies the female principle of desire, receptivity, nurturing, love, openness, and vulnerability.

> **The child's father-image creates the adult's ability to assert and to act.**
>
> **The child's experience of mom creates the adult's ability to be open, to be vulnerable, and to receive.**

Both male and female principles reside in every human. How they evolve and develop is unique to the individual, depending upon the child's healthy parenting.

If the child's innate trust in his parents is betrayed, issues of trust and betrayal may manifest throughout life. As an adult, he may trust the wrong people. Estranged from healthy selfhood, he may not even trust himself.

DAD: YOUR ABILITY TO ACT

If you experienced toxic dad, you might have difficulty defending yourself in a healthy way. Toxic parenting disconnects you from your healthy sense of self. You might be without legitimate entitlement to your desire—numb to what you truly want, feel, know, and need.

Not knowing what benefits you, you could wall-off and repress healthy action. Or, you could over-react to situations in an overly aggressive manner.

These unhealthy behaviors are twisted or skewed applications of a healthy, internal, male principle. Any affliction to your ability to act may be related to your childhood experience of dad.

If your relationship with your dad was conflicted by love and hate, you may suffer disabled will. You may be paralyzed by indecision, unable to act. Like Hamlet, you can get lost in the ontological uncertainty of "To be or not to be." You might compulsively over-analyze, dissecting each action ad infinitum, careening between loving and hating each decision. Simple choices can be overwhelming.

Another version of disabled will is being overly willful and aggressive. When the will wills itself, you may become an addict—to food, media, gambling, shopping, drugs, alcohol, or sex.

Conversely, you may be passive, letting others walk all over you. Internally, you may bounce between grandiosity and self-loathing.

MOM: YOUR ABILITY TO RECEIVE

Your ability to receive reflects your childhood experience of mom. Receiving requires an open hand and vulnerability. If mom were unsafe, you may not feel safe receiving the full-bounty of life's goodness. You may have trust issues with life itself.

Your ability to give is based on your experience of dad. A healthy adult has a balance of both giving and receiving. If you experienced toxic parenting as a child, it may affect both your ability to give and to receive as an adult.

If your mom was abandoning, you may co-dependently give too much and have difficulty receiving. You may self-erase, attracting tyrant/martyr scripts into your life. You may do life as work, demanding too much of yourself—unable to receive rest, rewards, pleasure, and vacations.

Conversely, you may be stingy and hoarding—afraid you will lose power if you open to release. Vulnerability may be difficult for you.

DAD/MOM: SPEAK AND LISTEN

Your ability to speak reflects your experience of dad. Your ability to listen is based on your experience of mom. A healthy adult has a balance of both listening and speaking—not too much or too little of either.

If you experienced toxic parenting as a child, you may experience difficulty either listening or speaking as an adult.

DAD/MOM: SEE AND HEAR

Notice your physical ability to see and to hear. They may also correlate with your dad/mom experience. Men in general are more visual, while women tend to be auditory.

Interestingly, hearing is your last sense to die. The ethereal God Sound ushers you through the birth canal to death realms on the other side of the Veil of earthly life. The feminine principle guides you into this life and into the next.

DAD/MOM: HEAD AND HEART

The quality of your head or thinking reflects your experience of dad. The quality of your heart is based on your experience of mom. A healthy adult has a balance of both head and heart—not too much or too little of either.

If you experienced toxic parenting as a child, you may experience difficulty either listening to your heart's true desire or your head's practical analysis as an adult. The two functions of open-hearted sensitivity and practical thinking may fog-out. You may be numb to your own feelings or beliefs.

Your head and heart may merge in hopeless confusion. "Do I want this or that?" may be a frequent internal script. You may muddle in hopeless confusion, unable to make a simple choice—alienated from your true self.

DAD/MOM: GOD AND LIFE

Across a lifetime, your experience of dad gets projected onto your God-concept or lack thereof. Your experience of mom is projected onto life.

Monitor your internal scripts regarding God and life. If you experienced abandonment, neglect, or unhealthy intrusion from dad/mom, you experienced child abuse. Your beliefs about life and God may correlate with your dad/mom experience.

Do you notice recurring scripts such as: "Life is not fair." "I never win." "There's no justice." "God doesn't care about me." "I'm alone here." "I just can't catch a break." "Bad luck follows me." "I'm a loser." "There is no one that I can trust." "Life is hopeless."

Negative internal scripts may be related to toxic parenting. You may want to continue the digestion process of toxic dad/mom to completion and resolution.

DAD/DAUGHTER AND MOM/SON

Esoteric tradition says before birth, when you designed your Soul Contract for your next life, you chose your parents for the lessons they can teach you.

Girls are magnetized to earth by the father. Boys are drawn by the mother. This is an interesting tidbit of information in passing, on the journey to deep, internal gender-essence.

EXPLORING YOUR FATHER

FATHERING QUESTIONNAIRE

To further explore the father archetype and the fathering you received, answer the following questions about your father.

1. How did/does your father feel about parenting? Does he carry fathering as a joy and a privilege? A drag and a burden? A job and a duty? A journey of discovery? Fun? A jailhouse?

2. What attitudes does he have about himself as father? Is he proud? Does he feel trapped? In over his head? Is he courageous? Complaining? A victim? Martyr? A tyrant? A spineless worm? Angry?

3. In a few words, describe your father's essence as a human being. Who is/was he? What archetype describes him? *See the chapter on "Jung's Gender Models" for a list of archetypes.*

Fathers and Fathering

4. What was the greatest gift your father gave you in life? What did he teach you?

5. What was the greatest wound, hurt, or rip-off that he gave you? What did he not give you that you needed?

6. What was broken inside your dad?

7. What was your father's biggest dream in life? How has your life copied or polarized against your father's dreams and ideals?

8. What was your father's greatest victory in life? His greatest fulfillment?

9. What was unfulfilled in your father's life? What was his greatest disappointment? What dream was unfulfilled? How does your life demonstrate your father's disappointments?

10. On your dad's deathbed, what was/will be his greatest failure? How does that affect you?

11. How has your life fulfilled your father's unfulfilled dreams? How do you redeem his loss? Have you lived your life to fulfill your father's dreams?

12. How are you living your dad's life? Are you living his dreams at the expense of your own?

13. How does your childhood father shape your world today?

14. Who are you most like—mom or dad? Who does your personality resemble? Who is/was your primary role-model for selfhood?

15. Is your identity authentically yours? Or, is it an iteration of your dad's identity? Are you enmeshed with your dad?

16. What can you do to achieve healthy separation?

17. How did your place in the birth order affect your experience of your father? Are you the family hero? Scapegoat? Mediator? Clown? Little Princess? Little Prince?

18. List the spontaneous associations that come to mind with the word "father." Don't judge. Just witness whatever comes up. Allow the good and bad to flow onto the page.

19. How did your father influence your perception of men and women? What is a man's proper place in the world? What is a woman's proper place in the world?

20. What false beliefs did your father teach you?

21. How did your dad feel about money? Working? His job? These are authority issues. How does your childhood dad affect you today? Do you hyper-achieve? Under-achieve? How do you manage money? Do you have money issues?

22. Did your father openly discuss problems? Money? Sex? Emotions? Religion? How did these discussions or lack thereof affect you in later life?

Fathers and Fathering

23. What were the family secrets? What were taboo subject that no one discussed? How do these taboos affect your life today?

24. Was your dad truthful? Honorable? Deceptive? A Liar? Was he faithful in his marriage?

25. How did your dad feel about the law? Rules? Government? People in power? God? How does your dad affect your feelings about laws and government? Powerful people? God? Did your dad break the rules? Do you have a recurring pattern of power, control, anger, and authority issues?

26. Did your dad have healthy boundaries? Did he say one thing and do another? Did he say "yes" and mean "no"? Were his rules fair? Did he stand by them? Did he play his rules against your mother's? Did he break the rules to look like the "good guy"?

27. Did your dad honor healthy boundaries with you sexually? Emotionally? Was he intrusive? A rager?

28. How did your dad resolve conflicts? Rage? Repress? Pretend? Victim? Tyrant? Abdicate? Openly discuss?

29. Did you witness your father abuse your mother in any way? Physically? Emotionally? Financially? Religiously?

30. Do you have victim/tyrant power issues in your life? In your self-talk?

31. Do you have calendar integrity? Do you keep your word? Do you feel there is never enough time? Are you a victim of

calendar-crunch and crazy-busy? Often, these are action-derangements from a lack of healthy fathering.

32. Do you have a healthy ability to act? To defend yourself? Do you speak when your rights are infringed?

33. Do you have healthy give and take in your relationships? Can you both listen and speak? Do you allow the other person to do all the talking?

34. Do you respect both head and heart approaches? Is only the analytical, scientific, left-brain approach correct?

35. Was your dad comfortable with emotions? Did he over or under express emotions? Was he a rager? Was he repressed? Too passive? Absent?

36. Did your dad name and validate your emotions, including your shadow emotions: anger, sadness, and fear? Do you express your anger in a healthy way? Do you over or under express your emotions?

37. How did your dad's modeling affect your health? Do you have good eyesight?

38. When you were a child, how did your dad behave in an emergency? Did you feel safe around your dad? Would your father stand and fight for you? Did he defend and protect you?

39. Was he safe to speak with regarding: Emotions? Money? Education? Jobs? Business? Politics? Sex? Religion? Food? Diet?

Fathers and Fathering

40. Did your dad know how to have fun? Did you have fun with him?

41. How did you feel about your dad in public? Were you proud of him? Ashamed? Could you trust him in public? Was he different in public from the way he behaved at home? Did he have two different personalities, public and private?

42. Did your dad have the ability to act? Do you have a healthy ability to act?

43. Did he effectively analyze and solve problems? Do you clearly analyze and solve problems?

44. Did your dad teach you to become yourself? Did he empower you? Did your father help you to construct healthy selfhood? *See the chapter on "Healthy Parenting" for healthy self-construction.*

45. How does your childhood dad affect the external events of your life today?

46. How has your childhood father affected the way you parent your own children?

47. How has your childhood father affected your choice of spouse?

48. How has your childhood father affected the way you treat your spouse?

49. Has toxic fathering helped to create the demise of your intimate relationships? Marriages?

50. Is it difficult for you to trust others? To get close to others? Are you able to sustain a long-term relationship?

After reflecting on your answers, if your father is alive, ask him the above questions. You may be surprised by his answers.

If your father is not available, step into his shoes. How do you think he would respond to each question?

YOUR DAD'S BEST QUALITIES

- List your dad's best qualities when you were a child. When you were a child, was your father:

    Loving? Safe? Strong? Protective? Wise? Intelligent? Powerful? Successful? Honest? Reliable? A good worker? Emotionally present? Easy to talk with? A good listener? A good talker? A good role model? An adult? A good mentor? Fun?

- How do these qualities reflect in you?
- How has he changed today?
- Is he the same person that he was when you were a child?

YOUR DAD'S WORST QUALITIES

- List your dad's worst qualities when you were a child. When you were a child, was your dad:

    Abandoning? Emotionally not present? Unavailable? Absent? Autocratic? Cruel? Angry? Sad? Fearful? Intimidated? Exhausted? Overworked? Unappreciated? Selfish? Self-indulgent? Indulgent to you? An addict? Absent?

- How do these qualities reflect in you?
- How has he changed today?
- Is he the same person that he was when you were a child?

YOUR INTERNAL DAD

- Examine your self-talk though the day. Listen to your internal father voice. Who is the father inside you? How do you self-parent? Does your internal father match the Essential Elements list in the "*Qualities of Fathering*" chapter?
- How does the fathering you experienced as a child play-out internally, in the voices in your head? How is your internal Critic related to your dad?
- Which of your dad's best qualities demonstrate in your self-fathering?
- Which of your dad's worst qualities demonstrate in your self-fathering?

WHAT CHANGES DO YOU WANT?

A legitimate defense mechanism to survive childhood can become an emotional jailhouse as an adult.

- What changes do you want from yourself psychologically?
- How do you want to change your internal self-talk?
- How do you want to change your internal self-parenting?
- How do you want to change the way you parent your children?
- What would you like to change in your current relationship with your dad?
- Do you need to ask for forgiveness?
- Do you need to grant forgiveness?
- What do you need to claim from the past?

- What do you need to release?
- Where, who, and how can you get the help you need to make changes, both for your family and for yourself?

For further support, there is a wonderful book list in the last chapter.

TAOISM'S GENDER MODELS

MALE-FEMALE ENERGIES

On my self-discovery quest, after unwinding the psychological complexities of childhood, I still needed to discover a healthy male model. I needed to design my internal selfhood, properly. I also wanted to find a healthy mate. I wondered what healthy male looked like in human form.

My determination to understand healthy behavior led me to the duality of all earthly life that endlessly flows between male and female energies. Exploring universal gender energies, I turned to Taoism which emerged from ancient China.

Taoist tradition teaches that the forces of life are dualized into yin and yang—the female principle and the male principle. While we are on earth, we are continuously immersed in both yin and yang energies. They are in constant, dynamic flux—balancing each other and contained within the larger whole.

YIN

Yin is the female principle. It is characterized by:

> Rest, sleep, hibernation, yielding, softness, slowness, receiving, non-doing, pleasure, surrender, darkness,

mystery, moisture, water, fertile, nurturing, love, safeness, mediator, submission, stillness, restoration, collecting, complexity, labyrinthine, obscurity, gentleness, vulnerability, receptivity, curves, diffused, internal, subjective, hidden, emotions, heart, empathy, indirect, peace, expansion, sound, night, relational, cooperation, whole-pattern oriented, society, tribe, left-side, co-operation, supportive, compromise, collaboration, home, winter.

The moon symbolizes the female with its many permutations, changes, and cycling. Moonlight is romantic and illusionary. Night is mysterious and full of shadows.

Negative yin with too much female energy corrupts the positive yin creating lassitude, weakness, exhaustion, dissipation, depression, sadness, or passivity.

YANG

Yang is the male principle characterized by:

Action, assertion, hardness, speed, giving, doing, will, discipline, aggressive, dominating, assertive, penetrating, brightness, fire, heat, fertilizer, protection, defending, guarding, strength, warrior, power, spending, direct, simple, clarity, straight-forward, external, objective, mental, straight-line, focused, speed, contraction, light, day, independent, competition, goal-oriented, self, hierarchy, right-side, leadership, outside world, summer.

The sun symbolizes the male with its directness, clarity, and single-pointed focus. Sunlight directly reveals concrete structures in the full light of day.

Negative yang with too much male energy deranges the positive yang creating anger, hyperactivity, mania, urgency, willfulness, or grandiosity. Too much yang creates the Doing Heart rather than the Receiving Heart that is open, soft, and balanced with yin energy. Too much male energy creates the day as a To Do List or a battle rather than receiving life as God's gift.

BALANCING

Taoist tradition says that for the culture to run smoothly, each family needs a woman to care for the home and a man to act in the world. This provides social stability.

In addition to external balance, the forces of yin (female principle) and yang (male principle) continually play inside each of us throughout the day. When yin and yang energies balance within, you transcend earthly duality into the peace of divine order. You become whole and natural. Aligned with right-order, your actions are empty of personal ego. There is harmony.

THE YIN-YANG WHEEL

Do you recall the Safeway market insignia? It is a circle with an S-curve inside. Half of the circle is solid black. The other half is solid white. This is similar to the Taoist Taijitu Wheel, the Yin-Yang Wheel.

The Wheel is a "diagram of ultimate power," the power that generates all life according to Taoist and ancient Chinese philosophy. It represents the concept of **opposites existing in harmony**. Taoist texts liken this image to a pair of fishes nestling head to tail against each other.

The circle itself represents the whole, while the black and white areas within it represent interacting parts or aspects of the whole. **The whole would be broken without its parts**. The white area, representing yang energy, is generally depicted as rising on the left; while the black(yin) area is shown descending on the right.

The image is designed to give the appearance of movement. Each area contains a large dot of the opposite color at its fullest point (near the zenith and nadir of the figure) to indicate how each will transform into the other.

When yang/white reaches extremes, it becomes heavy with excess, yang action-energy. This excess flips the Wheel, turning it until yin resting predominates. Similarly, extreme yin/black becomes yang, turning the Wheel again. If you spin the Wheel fast enough, it appears gray.

The Wheel of life turns in endless cycles of fullness. The opposites transmute and transform into new wholeness. By digesting each other, the yin and yang become each other in a newly informed oneness.

Each day, the extreme yang of daylight wanes into the extreme yin of night. Summer yang with its bright sunlight is filled with activity. The yang heat of summer becomes winter's yin of cold, darkness, and hibernation. The natural fullness of each essence—male and female—turns the Wheel of life.

The contracted yang seed becomes so filled with vital-force that it bursts open into the expansive, yin flower. Over time, the flower's fullness wanes and wilts into the ground, providing fertile soil for new life.

On the earthly plane of duality, female yin and male yang energies endlessly cycle back and forth. The Wheel always turns in the endless cycles of open/close, expand/contract, yin and yang.

Taken to its extreme, yin becomes death. Death becomes new life with each new generation. The extreme yang of the new baby grows old and dies. Life endlessly cycles. Life becomes death. Death becomes life. And, the Wheel spins. The local soap opera of earthly duality begins again!

In life's endless duality dance, the old becomes new again. The new eventually becomes old. Through the cycles of life and death turning the Wheel, divine order is created.

EXTREMES BECOME THE OPPOSITE

Excess yang becomes yin and vice versa. Extreme yang at its limit becomes stillness. For example, if you over-exert yourself, you become exhausted. To recuperate, you rest. Stillness generates yin.

After rest, you are ready to go again, into another cycle of yang activity. Extreme yin at its limit becomes yang.

Activity and stillness alternate. Each is the basis of the other. **Too much stillness/yin or activity/yang creates derangement of the natural balance. The Wheel turns to restore order.**

The alternating and combining of yang and yin energies generate all earthly life according to Chinese philosophy. The yin-yang principle of bipolarity is the basic ordering principle, the cosmic first principle. The polarity is embraced by the unity of the whole circle. The polarities are fundamentally non-polar, always in dynamic flux which is the state of life.

The key to health is movement and continuous energy exchange dialoguing between the two extremes. When the yin/yang dialogue stops, earthly death ensues.

WHOLENESS

In Taoism, the co-existence of opposites occurs in harmony due to the greater value of the whole. The dynamic of opposites within the larger whole is the natural order.

Valuing natural order, Taoists are excellent at detachment, surrender, and empty-ego. Rather than the instant gratification of personal desire, they play the long-game honoring nature's design. They know that polarized ego-battles are transitory. Balancing energies and co-creating the whole win in the end. Energy exchange is the natural way.

They value going with the flow of universal principles and serving the whole. Because of the Yin-Yang Wheel, they transcend rigid self-righteous duality into oneness.

Native American Indians call this ego transcension "walking a mile in the other person's moccasins." Christians say, "Love the other as you love yourself." They also transcend polarized entrenchment into the greater good of the unity principle.

Living in a family, parenting children teaches this same wisdom. You learn to see the other person's view. You value it, rather than judge it. This expands your identity into a larger wholeness.

Understanding the Yin-Yang Wheel is an insurance policy against imbalance. Taoists see the good of the whole as enduring beyond personal life. They surrender to the greater good as honor, not sacrifice. Families are where we learn these team-building skills.

ASTROLOGY AND YIN-YANG BALANCE

In studying Taoist models, I noticed an imbalance of excess yang energy in contemporary culture. We are living hyper-stimulated, stress-filled lives. Society has lost healthy balance. The healthy female-principle, yin is devalued—both internally in self-talk and externally in the world.

The following is a quote from astrologer Terry Lamb's wonderful work, "Planetary Cycles," www.terrylamb.net. She discusses the world of yin and yang, showing how we can tap into the blessings of the yin cycle.

> Yin is a primal power, equal in strength to yang, complementary and interpenetrating. Yin is the field or opening that receives the seed of yang. Yin's power to accept and give things form is unlimited.
>
> Through yin, we gain the power to give things form. If you're having trouble manifesting, you are probably out of balance toward yang, with underdeveloped yin. If you have too little yin in your life, be more receptive. Yield sincerely to each thing that comes to you, nourishing it (or redirecting it if it is out of balance).
>
> Yin uses the instrument of time for its development. Yin works through the collection, concentration, storage, and organization of energy.
>
> During a time of yin development, accept the slow pace, but keep your sense of purpose. If you try to rush things, it will take longer because it throws yin out of balance when we rush. Do whatever presents itself to be done without judging it.
>
> Test your ideas. Let go of the past, but don't shirk responsibilities. Be calm and confident. Don't take the lead—allow yourself to be led. This releases transformative energy. Accept that some processes and energies are hidden and should remain that way until they emerge on their own.

Yin is the energy of the earth signs: Taurus, Virgo, and Capricorn—especially in grand trine. Terry recommends, in a yin cycle, "Don't expect a Big Change to rescue you from your dilemmas; do expect that by collecting yin energy you will overcome the obstacles that you have been dealing with. If you do the work patiently and calmly, you will be able to grow everything you want in your Sacred Garden."

GENERATIONAL CYCLES

Periods of history operate in cycles of the Yin-Yang Wheel. Each period experiments with a particular style and takes it to its fullest extreme. Then, a grassroots movement arises to newly discover the polar opposite. It becomes the norm until its cycle is complete.

The Wheel turns and a newly defined opposite becomes vogue. The duality dance endlessly cycles.

Each generation has its own Soul Contract and developmental agenda in the evolution of human consciousness. However, the cycles of discovery are archetypal in their repetition.

For example, each generation rediscovers war and gender; art and science; love and relationship; alone and together. However, each generation brings its unique stamp to the human journey—hopefully advancing the Human Experiment in some way.

War and peace are cycles of the Yin-Yang Wheel turning. The exhaustion of war demands rest and renewal. After rest, there is new energy for action and to solve new problems.

With the current imbalance of gender energy, there is a need to advance the male-female dialogue. It is time to bring the new order as the evolutionary Wheel turns.

Yin and yang recalibration is the sacred calling. We need to collect our yin.

JUNG'S GENDER MODELS

BEHAVIORAL PATTERNS

I expanded my understanding of male and female energies by exploring Jung's social roles and behavioral patterns. Carl Jung is one of the giants of psychology. He originated archetypal psychology, which examines recurring experiences in the human journey.

ARCHETYPES

An archetype is a behavioral pattern that emerges across cultures, regions, and periods in history. It symbolizes a behavior or role that is intrinsic to the human experience regardless of when, where, or how you live. It is encoded in the human DNA, in the collective unconscious inside every human.

A full range of archetypes—both good and bad, heroes and villains—exists inside everyone. Archetypes illumine what it is to be human. The father archetype is the symbol of authority. The mother archetype represents nurturing.

To familiarize yourself with archetypes, get a Tarot deck. There, you will discover a fabulous parade of recurring images that march across the human drama. Tarot archetypes include:

Fathers and Fathering

> Magician, high priestess, priest, politician, king, queen, lover, child, family, artist, builder, apprentice, workman, warrior, real estate, merchant, wealth, money, birth, love, celebration, creation, death, destruction, rebirth, martyr, addiction, burden, grief, loss, hard work, perseverance, anger, fear, unknown, frustration, orphan, destitution, struggle, greed, balance, hope, philanthropy, news, communication, severity, meditation, temperance, hermit, retreat, solitude, hero, strength, baby, sex, fertility, luck, justice, surrender, transcension, devil, transformation, hero, the world, success, moon, sun, fate, spirituality, practical life, beliefs, dominion.

Astrology provides another showcase of gods and archetypal essences. Here are some of them:

> Sun's purpose; Moon's nurturing; Earth's renewal; Mercury's communication; Venus' love; Mars' assertion; Saturn's discipline; Jupiter's luck; Uranus' revolution; Pluto's regeneration; Neptune's spirituality; Vesta's perfectionism; Ceres's mothering; Athena's wisdom; Hygeia's health; Vulcan's protection; and Juno's partnership.

The pantheons of ancient Egypt, Greece, Rome, and India further reveal the richness of archetypal life in the complex intrigues of the many gods. Some popular Egyptian gods include:

> Horus, the falcon protector god, accessing the many worlds; Isis, the ideal wife and mother; Ra, the life-giving sun god; Anubis, the jackal-headed god of the afterlife; and Sekhmet, the lion goddess of war and healing.

The Hindu pantheon contains:

> Brahma, the creator god; Vishnu, the preserver; Shiva, the destroyer; Shakti, the change-agent and goddess of creative power; Kali, the empowerment goddess of the first creation before light; Krishna, the child-god of play, fun, and devotion; Rama, the god of virtue and duty; Lakshmi, the goddess of beauty, prosperity, and good luck; Ganesha, the elephant god of wisdom who removes obstacles.

YOUR ARCHETYPES

It is useful to identify yourself, your partner, and your parents in this parade of archetypes. Which archetype defines you? Which role or image defines your father? Your mother? Your partner? Your internal scripts? Your internal selves? The type of day you experienced today?

Use archetypes to distill and reduce life experiences to manageable icons and symbols. Roles change as your time in life changes. Identifying archetypes brings clarity and choices of how to be male and female.

Use archetypes to **cast the movies in your mind**, translating external events into useful psychological elements. The value of creating **mind-movies** is to consciously identify the parts of your life. Casting heroes and villains in melodramas opens your thinking.

Archetypes shift you into the impersonal land of universal myths and pantheons. You feel less alone when you see the long march of time—realizing how many other humans have walked the same path as yours. When you achieve distance, you gain freshness and freedom.

Archetypes help you to ascend your God Ladder and broaden your perspective. You drop your defensive ego. Mind-movies help you to laugh at yourself and life. Laughter transmutes pain to power.

Through archetypes, you gain detachment and insight. You see your role, your personal development, your time in life, your identity, and your relationships—in a larger context. You learn to take life seriously, but not personally. Accessing soul levels, archetypes provide wisdom to deal with life's problems.

In relationships, by identifying a person's archetype, you can relate to him more clearly. Knowing his archetype connects you with his design, so you can have realistic expectations. You can better serve both the other and yourself.

Archetypes help you to see life impersonally, through the eyes of the soul. A person's archetype reveals his Soul Contract, which is his mission for a particular incarnation. With Soul Glasses, you realize that each person is simply playing the part assigned to him by Central Casting before birth.

Archetypes help you to digest both earthly and divine life.

NAMING WITHOUT BLAMING

Archetypes move us from blaming toxic parents to simply objectively naming each person's journey—both yours and mom/dad's.

When you see parents through the archetypal eyes of Divine Mother/Father, you see with universal eyes. You witness your mom/dad as a parent sees a child. Your parents become vulnerable children, searching for their way in life, just like the rest of us.

Judgment Day is left to God. It goes far beyond mortal ken.

Before birth, you co-created your Soul Contract with your soul and divine guides. You chose your exact parents to learn specific lessons from them. Sometimes, we learn through opposites. We can learn right-action by seeing another person's mistakes.

While there are legitimate victims from the earthly view, from the divine view, there are no victims since you selected your parents.

It is empowering to awaken through archetypes and to become conscious of your childhood journey. Naming your experience without blaming yourself or others brings awakening and clarity.

Then, you can reclaim lost power. Freed from the past, you can design a future based on your true self.

ANIMA AND ANIMUS

While there are various schools of Jungian thought, archetypal psychology says that everyone has both an animus which is the active male principle; and an anima, the receptive female principle. To be happy and healthy you must develop both, your active and receptive sides. Otherwise, you become unbalanced.

For example, if you are a woman and have too much receptive energy, you can become a subservient doormat with no entitlement. You might lack healthy boundaries. Without a healthy sense of self, you lose your power of "No." You can become absorbed in your partner's world at the expense of your own. You might become codependent—giving in order to get—lacking personal value. You can wander in confusion, lost in a masochistic muddle.

Too much receptive, female, yin energy creates sloth and torpor—the inability to act.

On the other hand, if you are a man and contain too much active energy, you can become overly aggressive. Instead of healthy containment, you might physicalize your emotions in gratuitous fights and power struggles. You could regress to a power-mongering dictator. Without healthy limits, you can become egocentric. You risk becoming a sadistic barbarian.

Too much active, male, yang energy creates anger and action-addiction—the inability to rest.

INTEGRATION

To avoid doormat or barbarian status, you must engage the opposite gender-principle within you. With internal balance of active male and receptive female energies, yang and yin, you have the ability to take healthy action.

You openly receive new information. Your actions are clear, conscious, and centered. You use the skills of healthy selfhood for healthy action, including:

> Boundaries and limits; entitlement; self-interview; objective naming skills; truth-telling; communication; active-listening with empathy; confrontation; impulse control; enlistment skills; and conflict resolution.

You monitor both the male and female forces that naturally co-exist inside you, as you apply right-action. You balance your internal anima and animus, receptive and active energies.

For example, if you want to develop your receptive female, you might study dance, art, cooking, meditation, dreams, nature walks, or moon-howling. If you want to develop your active male nature, you might study martial arts, football, sports, money, running, the history of war, carpentry, auto mechanics, or mathematics.

Jung said that your male and female, anima and animus evolve over time. Their values morph through four stages: 1) pleasure/desire physicality 2) worldly contribution 3) moral and intellectual pursuits 4) final stage female wisdom in Sophia and male action in Hermes the messenger of the gods.

Your anima and animus digest and mediate the lower three rungs of your God Ladder: your physical, emotional, and mental bodies. Your anima and animus evolve the dialogue between your conscious and unconscious minds. Your earthly anima and animus are links to the divine rungs on your God Ladder.

We need both male animus and female anima to fully enjoy life's party. Women bring the curves; men bring the straight lines—physically, emotionally, mentally, and spiritually.

YOUR SOUL AND YOUR SPIRIT

Jung says that the female anima at its highest level provides access to your soul. As a mystic, I see that your earthly anima and animus prepare you to meet your divine equipment.

Using God Ladder terms, your male and female principles manifest in your divine nature as your soul and your spirit. These are higher vibrational realms than your earthly equipment.

We discuss your entire God Ladder in greater detail in the chapter on *The Wise Man and the Wise Woman*.

YOUR SOUL

Your earthly anima is a gateway to your divine soul.

The ultimate receptive female, your soul sees the larger picture beyond earthly life. Through her, you access the higher rungs of your God Ladder: your intuition, soul, spirit, and Universal God Source.

Like a loving Divine Mother, your soul nurtures, supports, and encourages you. She gives you internal refuge, renewal, and supply to face daily living. She is your muse, refueling and inspiring you with transcendent energy for your earthly journey.

Your soul is the still, small voice of conscience within you. You often reach her by listening to your heart. She is the female energy inside you manifesting in the divine octaves of your God Ladder.

By consciously connecting with your soul, Divine Mother teaches you healthy behavior. She models healthy mothering. Regardless of your earthly parents, you can always receive healthy mothering and yin supply through Divine Mother.

YOUR SPIRIT

Your earthly animus is an aspect of your divine spirit, Divine Father.

The male principle helps you to take action in the world. Through him, you assert yourself for success. With left-brain analysis, he guides you to problem-solving solutions.

Divine Father gives you courage and strength. Your divine male activates your healthy warrior to fulfill your heart's true desire. He teaches you to defend and to protect your healthy boundaries, entitlement, and selfhood. He helps you to fight for justice. He is the male energy inside you at the divine vibration of your spirit on the God Ladder.

Divine Father demonstrates divine truth and healthy self-transcension. By consciously connecting with your divine male, Divine Father teaches you healthy parenting. He models healthy fathering. Regardless of your earthly father, through Divine Father you can access healthy male energy.

RIGHT-ACTION

Right-action is the marriage of anima and animus, yin and yang, male and female principles, divine and earthly equipment. The anima is a listening function for receiving guidance. The animus is a doing function, providing the ability to act on the information.

For right-action, you need both—listening to your soul; then, designing the proper response to fit each occasion. In daily reality, you continuously receive inner guidance from your soul and spirit. You translate their wisdom down your God Ladder into right-action in the world.

If you stop listening to your internal female, you risk unhealthy action. You may become overly male—acting-out unhealthy, aggressive misbehavior.

Conversely, if all you do during the day is loll about, dreaming, and conjuring with your internal female—lethargy rules your external world. You may be paralyzed by inaction.

Do you push too hard? Not hard enough? Either extreme can reflect toxic parenting with its ensuing imbalance of male/female energies.

Life has endless cycles of construction and deconstruction. They require that you know how to access both your internal male and female—your spirit and your soul, your animus and anima, your ability to act and your ability to rest. Through your Divine Mother and Divine Father, you can learn healthy self-care and self-parenting.

MALE ACTION-DERANGEMENT

ACTION ADDICTION

If you experienced toxic parenting as a child, as an adult, you may over-achieve, have an inability to rest, or need constant activity. The distraction of hyper-activity is a defense mechanism against being present in true self-discovery. Action addiction is a mis-application of the male principle.

Do you avoid silence and stillness? Or, do you have periods of rest and non-doing throughout your day? Do you stop to meditate, pray, reflect, or write in your journal? Or, is your day packed with non-stop events? Are you connected to yourself, internally naming your emotions? Or, do all your circuits externalize to other people and outside activity?

If you are an action addict, it may not have been safe for you to be yourself as a child. Your authentic, integrated self might be foreign and undeveloped inside you. It could even terrify you. Your healthy ability to act in a balanced way could be paralyzed.

Action addiction cripples your ability to act in a healthy way—including both rest and activity. Crazy-busy and time-urgency lock you inside arrested development.

Action is an expression of the male-principle, yang energy. Healthy action is centered—empty of ego-attachment and pushing. It is clean and clear energy in alignment with divine order. The source of the action is anchored in the impersonal world of the divine realm, rather that false-godding from earthly self.

> **Feeling like a hunted animal—a victim of calendar-crunch—is not healthy living.**
>
> **Feeling guillotined by the ticking clock is another form of internalized victim/tyrant consciousness from childhood abuse.**

Unhealthy action energy is unbalanced, with too much or too little expression. It is ego driven—with too much or too little self. The energy also can be twisted in misapplication.

Being lost in endless "achievements" and action with too much excitement does violence to your nervous system. In a short time, you become addicted to your own adrenalin. Your body literally forgets how to rest. The natural becomes unnatural to you. You become an action addict in the derangement of your healthy male-principle.

Action addiction fragments and scatters your divine energies. It takes an ax to the center of your being. Self-shredding and decimation is not soul-centered action.

Action abuse is common in contemporary culture. Action derangement can become so unbalanced that you don't make time for basic needs like rest. You can actually feel guilty for resting! Soon, your body can forget how to rest.

Losing a healthy sleep-cycle disconnects you from natural biorhythms. Soon, you lose healthy eating patterns and begin stress eating. Getting 8-10 hours of sleep each night is essential for higher productivity, more energy, and less stress.

Without your soul's conscience to guide you, you can abuse healthy boundaries with excessive eating, stimulants, and busy-ness. There's no healthy internal adult in charge of setting limits for your body, emotions, mind, or behavior.

STRESS

Stress changes your biochemistry and remodels your nervous system. When your attention darts interminably from one project to the next, your body normalizes to stress.

In the stress trance, you forget where healthy normal went. You desensitize to pain. There is no refuge or renewal. The panic of living in a survival mode creates hormonal imbalance, opening the body to disease.

Chronic stress disconnects the neural systems of the brain that are wired to the prefrontal cortex where conscience and healthy shame reside. The prefrontal cortex is not completely developed until twenty-five years old. It filters incoming data so good judgment prevails, putting the brakes on out-of-control emotions, such as rage.

Habituating to hyper-activity is hazardous. Stress and crime are connected. Stress and disease are connected. Stress and child abuse are related.

HYPER-BUSY

Hyper-busy, stress-riddled behavior has become a national epidemic. The computer scatters and fragments our attention. Besieged by cyber stimulation and beleaguered by excess information, we overload. Driving while phoning, people risk their lives multi-tasking. Family life and dinner etiquette evaporate, decimated by cell phones and crowded schedules.

There's an avalanche of input stressing our nervous systems. The current zeitgeist can be expressed by the film title: *Stop the World, I Want to Get Off!*

Are you hyper-vigilant, like a rat darting through a maze of action-items, multi-tasking throughout the day? Do you feel driven by your To Do List? Are you chasing endless activities?

Action addiction is tantamount to taking an ax and shattering healthy selfhood. You may be avoiding meeting your true and natural self—your male and female—living in peace and balance.

Your natural self is much, much less than all the external hoo-haa. It is blessed ordinariness.

DISABLED WILL

Too much action can reflect disabled will—an injured, internal male-principle. Excessive willfulness is self-will run riot. In this action derangement, the will wills itself.

With a broken, internal male, you frantically dash through activities. Rather than engaging in measured, deliberate, continual dialogue with your soul, you are driven by self-will. Soon, egotistical willfulness multiplies, breaking the law of healthy, human limits.

Self-willing is a soul atrocity. Your inflated ego decimates your soul connection, your conscience, and your internal female. Grandiosity replaces God and the natural order. Without healthy shame and healthy limits, it is impossible to discern right-action from the hypnotic trance of doing.

Disabled will can be a symptom of child-abuse and a twisted, love/hate father archetype. Tyrannical grandiosity victimizes and subjugates the internal female. Perhaps, you witnessed an imbalance of male/female power in your childhood.

Wanton willfulness can be an attempt to disguise powerlessness. Willfulness compensates for feeling helpless and hopeless. These false beliefs can emerge if the child feels unsafe and unprotected by a healthy male. Victim/tyrant issues can ensue, sometimes across a lifetime.

Excessive swearing can be an indicator of wanton willfulness and displaced anger—an injured male principle. You can modulate the toxic energy discharge of swearing by finding a similar word or sound that expels the frustration from your body. Growling can sometimes work. It can get you laughing which unbinds the attachment to negative emotion.

Another simple remedy for male-principle abuse is empathy. Listening with an open heart and naming the other person's emotions engages your soul and increases your yin energy. Shifting your focus to help another person can break the mind-lock of willfulness.

In the ultimate yin rx, enlist your soul to listen to the angry, frustrated, victim voices inside you. "I'm overworked and underpaid. There's not enough time or energy to get everything done. No one ever helps me. I'm alone." Ask your soul to moderate and resolve your internal victim voices.

Being an adult means dealing with limits. Life is about facing hard choices. Right-action involves trade-offs and compromises. Resolve angry, internal voices, rather than displace the toxic energy in action abuse.

Perhaps, internal conflict resolution means learning to live with imperfection. Maybe the solution is to do a little piece of the job every day, rather than doing it all at once. If you are overwhelmed, maybe you need to learn to ask for help. Find Buddha's Middle Way as you learn to balance action abuse with healthy action.

Another popular action-abuse is perfectionism. In your willfulness and false beliefs are you trying to do everything perfectly? Are you a prisoner of perfectionism. As a remedy, try asking, "Is it good enough?" "Have I done my part?" As you face the limits of your earthly self, you can learn to let that be enough. You can let go and let God do the rest.

THE MONEY-GOD

Serving the money-god in today's world reinforces male-principle derangement. The action sickness of money grabbing and fixating on career undermines healthy selfhood. As the poet William Wordsworth says, "The world is too much with us; late and soon, getting and spending, we lay waste our powers."

Imagine waking-up tomorrow to discover that the cultural values are wisdom, instead of the money-god. The coinage of the kingdom is wisdom rather than cash!

Imagine if the divine female-principle (soul) marries the earthly male-principle (action). In the conjoining of heaven and earth, yin wisdom and yang action unite. The Wise Man and the Wise Woman are born.

If wisdom is the coinage of the culture, how does your job change? How does society change? How do your relationships change? How does your sense of yourself change? How does your stress level change!

The nation suffers from a glut of yang materialism, while starving for yin spirituality and the soul's wisdom. Albert Einstein said, "It has become appallingly clear that our technology has surpassed our humanity....Without wisdom, humanity is in danger of destroying itself." Carl Jung added, "Twenty-first century human beings will be spiritual or will not be at all."

TODAY'S CULTURAL IMBALANCE

Too much doing can create chaos. Similarly, too much non-doing can create chaos. Any imbalance of male or female principles is unhealthy.

> **Sadly, today's world is crazy-busy with a male-principle derangement that is perpetrating violence to the soul.**

We are in danger of becoming human doings—soulless robots—rather than human beings. To fully digest life, everyone needs the power to act and the time to reflect.

The natural rhythm of action and rest is as important as day and night. All life on earth follows this yin/yang pattern of awake/asleep; birth/death; inhale/exhale.

The soul's voice is the Divine Feminine. It comes from the heart. The male action-principle is an aspect of Divine Father. It comes from the head. Right living involves both head and heart co-creating in balance.

Both healthy, internal mother and father are needed to monitor your inner scripts and to parent your inner children. Healthy male and female-principles are essential to divine order in your inner village of voices.

Without healthy childhood parenting, many of us are lacking healthy gender models. **Male action-derangement reflects a lack of healthy father images to guide us in our society.**

YIN BALANCE

Today, the world needs a heavy dose of yin to balance its male action-addiction. The medicine for yin is rest, inactivity, stillness, meditation, silence, listening to your soul, opening your heart. Embrace your yin entitlement and you will emerge a new person. True happiness will return to your kingdom.

The female archetype is the progenitor of life. She brings nurturing and self-care; softness and quietude.

The visual cyber-world of videos and computers are sight-intensive, male activities. They reinforce willfulness and power-games. By contrast, hearing is connected to surrender, vulnerability, and openness—the receptive female principle.

The lost art of listening in families and in government reflects a deficit of yin energy in the culture. Listening with your heart is an important skill.

Helen Keller was born both blind and deaf. She said, "If you lose sight, you lose touch with things. If you lose hearing, you lose touch with people." Loss of nourishing social engagement is the highest indicator for morbidity. Simply hanging-out with friends regularly can balance your yin. It is good for your health.

> **Keep a soft heart. Listen to quiet, relaxing music. Enjoy the silence. Receive the gift of stillness throughout the day. Breathe. Smile. Count your blessings.**
>
> **These simple skills will balance your yin against the action-driven culture.**

Meditating with your inner male and female, your animus and anima can help you to regain sanity. Have your action-self dialogue with your restful-self. Some days, they may even argue with each other.

Observe their struggle. Self-witnessing can help you to objectively name your experience.

Why is your inner male afraid of rest? What terrifies him? Is he afraid of extinction?

Sometimes these inner scripts are buried in the subconscious mind. Through meditation, I discovered that during my birth, my mother's nurse said, "Push or you'll die!" I subconsciously carried this script into my adult life. This script was not even mine! When I became conscious of my inner struggle, a burden was lifted from me.

With balance, you can awaken from the collective hallucination of action derangement.

HEALING STRESS

The imbalance of twisted male-principle is both in the culture and internally within you. When your mind is jetting like popcorn in every direction and you want to slow down, here are some simple recommendations. Stepping out of time will help you to balance action addiction. Grabbing some healthy me-time will feed your yin goddess.

Close your eyes and the world of form disappears. External distractions go away. You enter the Void of deconstructed form, blessed emptiness. Oh, what a relief it is! The chaos stops. The frenzy quiets. This is the ultimate yin, the feminine energy, the divine embrace.

Brain studies show, the moment you close your eyes, you move from the action mode of beta brainwaves into the relaxed state of alpha and meditation.

Sadly, the ingrained Puritan work-ethic shames us for non-doing. In today's action-deranged world, rest is foreign and difficult to achieve. It doesn't sell well. There are no admen enticing you to the Nothingness. The non-doing is not a big product-buy.

When you open your eyes, the world of form clamors for attention. Mammon and the money-god beckon. The To-Do Lust returns.

To remedy stress and to increase healthy yin in your life, use the following simple suggestions. They will help to restore balance.

Choose the exercise that suits you. Practice regularly, 5-10 minutes/day. Remember, even the Creator rested on the seventh day!

1. **Witnessing Thoughts**. Sit or lie with your eyes closed. Notice the jetting thoughts. As thoughts enter, just let them dissolve, like bubbles floating downstream. Don't attach your attention to any of them. Don't grasp after them. Don't judge if a thought enters. Simply watch it, as a detached observer. You are a spectator. Witness the thoughts floating through your mind and disappearing. Just let them float through you.

2. **Connected Breaths**. Lie in a comfortable position. Without gasping, simply inhale fully. Exhale fully. If thoughts enter, don't judge. Simply return to focus on your breathing. All that exists is your breathing. Inhale. And exhale. Hear your breath enter and leave your body. Feel the coolness of the fresh air enter when you inhale. Feel the heat at the end of your nose as you exhale. Practice 50-100 connected breaths every day.

3. **Turn the Wheel**. Using your connected breathing, add the visual image of a wheel turning from the top of your head to the bottom of your feet. See the wheel in golden Light. Inhale down the front of your body. Exhale up the back of your body.

4. **Visual Imagery**:
    a. Imagine wafting downward, falling like a feather on the Breath of God. Relax into the embrace of deep yin.
    b. Imagine yourself falling backwards into the Arms of God. Let go and let God support you now. Feel the relaxation taking you deeper into God's Embrace.
    c. Feel the Hands of God supporting you. The same Hands that hold the earth in space are holding you now. Just let go and let God support you. Feel the weights lift off your body as you relax into the Hands of God. Relax and let God carry you.
    d. Imagine 10,000 tiny angel hands massaging you. All

the cares of the day are soothed and smoothed away in their loving touch.

   e. Feel yourself floating on a warm ocean wave of Divine Love. With every inhale, the wave rises. With every exhale, the wave falls. Inhale. Exhale. Inhale. Exhale. Inhale. Exhale. Rocking back and forth on a warm wave in an ocean of Divine Love.

5. **Sectional Relaxation of the Body**.

   a. Just for now, tell all the cares of the day to wait outside the door while you relax. You will deal with them later.

   b. Inhale relaxation to all the muscles around your eyes, ears, nose, mouth, jaws, and forehead. Even your tongue is relaxed. With each exhale, feel the tension release.

   c. Inhale relaxation to the muscles of your neck, shoulders, arms, and hands. Inhale, relax. Exhale, release tension. See the tension leaving, floating away, and dissolving into outer space.

   d. Inhale relaxation to the muscles and systems of your chest, abdomen, buttocks, legs, and feet. Even your anus is relaxed. Inhale relaxation. Exhale released tension.

   e. Remain in the peace and quiet of relaxation for a number of minutes. Dwell there. Let it be.

6. **The Gateway University Yantra**. Use the Gateway Sri Yantra (see www.GatewayUniversity.org) to gaze in one-pointed, diffused gaze at the center of the mandala for 5-10 minutes/day. Simply witness the color and light changes. Don't judge. Just dissolve in the Light. If your mind wanders, bring it back to the dot in the center of the yantra.

7. **Zen Meditation**. Go to your local Buddhist monastery to learn Zen. This is excellent for quieting the nervous system and stilling the mind. Over a period of time, Zen meditation will teach you to actually stop your mind. The panic will dissolve as you learn a quiet mind.

8. **Vipassana Meditation**. Buddhist Vipassana can be learned quickly. It is also called insight or mindfulness meditation. Vipassana helps you to quiet the mind, to develop your witness point, and to replace lost yin. It strengthens your detached observation, unhooking your identity from worldly din. It is invaluable for balance in daily living. Read any of Jack Kornfield or Joseph Goldstein's wonderful books on the subject.

9. **Rigorous Exercise**. Remember extreme yang becomes yin. You can transmute the tension and negative energy in your body through 20-30 minutes of rigorous exercise every day.

10. **Hiking in Nature**. Take an hour a day, walking in the sunshine and fresh air. Let Sky Father free your spirit from the mind-trap of excessive yang. Earth Mother will ground you in healthy yin.

11. **Blessings Basket**. At the end of each day, harvest the gifts. Collect the blessings you received—a phone call, an email, a joke, a friend's support, your victories, and successes. Even little things count. Let the full bounty of the Beauty Way smile upon you. Don't waste, spill, or squander the gifts of the day. Harvest them in your Blessings Basket.

12. **Listen to Peaceful Music**.

13. **Relax Your Shoulders**. Are you "shouldering" too many shoulds and burdens? Carrying too much responsibility? Can you delegate some duties? Can you release guilt and accept the limits of being human?

14. **Practice Simpler Living**. Miles van der Rohe, the famous minimalist architect said, "Less is more." His expression invites a more relaxed nervous system. Create space in your home. Weed-out your closets. Things take energy. Reduce the clutter.

15. **Half-Day of Silence**. Each month, dedicate 6 consecutive hours to a speech fast. Remember "Less is more."

16. **The Gateway University Audio Collection** (for more information here, see www.GatewayUniversity.org). Use the following Gateway classes for daily relaxation:

- The Divine Gaze
- Soul-Infusion
- Soul Installation
- Soul-Infusion Gift
- Soul Gentling
- Relaxation and Guided Imagery

EMBRACING THE SACRED FEMININE

Humanity stands at a perilous crossroad in history. To survive, we must embrace our souls and the Divine Feminine. Both men and women conspire in abandoning healthy yin. Both genders dismember their sacred female in the crazy-busy.

To advance the Human Experiment, it's time to shift our consciousness from excessive, male-energy imbalance. The male societal model is hierarchical, based on competition. By contrast, the female model is tribal, based on cooperation.

To rectify the current action-derangement, we must move our consciousness from "me" to "we". We must evolve beyond worshipping the money-god and separation consciousness. Somehow, we must evolve from competition and exclusion into cooperation and co-creation.

Clearly, the healthy female-principle needs renovation! This renewal is the mandate for the next cycle that is emerging. A healthy dose of yin and Divine Feminine is needed for balance.

MY STRESS PRAYER

In my recovery from action addiction, my Guides continually repeat:

Dear One,

Your stress is because you are pushing. Rather than opening your heart to receive the day, you are 'doing' the day. You push away our offerings, ignoring our gifts. You throw our gifts in the gutter when you don't receive them.

Fathers and Fathering

When you get lost in willing your own agenda, it is an act of violence against your sacred self. You need a partnership with us every moment of the day. We will help you to realize your dreams. Listen to us. Let us guide you. We will move your action forward in Divine Order.

It is safe now to open and to receive. We will not betray you. Trust us. Surrender into our love. Keep a soft heart. Let us in. We will help you. We live to serve you.

My Guides said that without realizing it, I was holding tension in my body, unbalancing my energy-shields. They said, "Practice being focused and centered without pushing. Having a focused mind is different from being willfully driven."

Chastened, I adopted a new prayer:

Divine Mother,

I stand here with my arms wide-open to receive your gifts. Soften my heart. Make the slowness safe. Make it safe for me to receive. Make it safe for me to breathe.

Help me to let go, knowing you will lift me. Open me to receive the blessed sacrament of each moment in my day.

Soothe my brokenness. Teach me to love the darkness free. Hold me in your divine embrace. Enfold me with your grace.

Let me rest in your arms, trusting the silence. Open my heart to listen to your wisdom. Protect and direct me. Guide me in the Wisdom Way.

When trouble comes, help me to remember that I always lay my head on the pillow at the end of the day. Lead me to walk with balance, no longer alone.

And so it is.

The more hassled you feel, the more you need the sacred space. Hopeless and helpless internal scripts signal the need for Divine Embrace. At these moments, surrender your brokenness into the arms of Divine Mother. Allow her to lift you.

SOCIETAL GENDER LIES

GENDER ROLES AND GENDER ESSENCE

In my wrestling with gender, through Taoist yin/yang energies to Jungian male/female archetypes, I felt there was something missing. These gender models addressed external social-roles. My inner hound-dog for truth sniffed there was something more.

There is a distinction between external, societal gender-role and internal, deep gender-essence. Somewhere, there's a lie in what society teaches us about how to be a man and how to be a woman. External gender roles belie deep inner knowing.

In my search to clarify dad/mom, I continued to ask "What is the deep gender-essence?" The Yin-Yang Wheel and Jung's anima-animus are valuable tools. They provide good male/female references points for achieving balance and integrity, both in the culture and personally.

However, there was still something missing inside me. There was a deep roar, a rawness of deep, primal, internal gender-essence crying for discovery. It had not yet been addressed. It demanded to be heard.

I plunged deeper in my exploration of what it means to be male and female. What was I trying to uncover? I meticulously sorted the layers of what society had done to me, what my family of origin had done to me, what my family of creation had done to me, and what my past lives had done to me as a woman. Remember, I'm a mystic and a psychologist!

Until I sorted the wreckage of my broken selves, I couldn't see my true, deepest gender-essence to rescue it from the rubble. Like a baby crying for mother, I could hear and feel my deep essence. I knew it was there. I was determined to find it. My search continued.

FEMALES IN FILM

Films often reveal the collective search for gender balance. Neptune rules the collective soul and also films.

In today's films, women often search for their lost male energy. However, sadly heroines too often copy twisted, male-modeled violence and abuse of power. Notice "Kill Bill," "Crouching Tiger, Hidden Dragon," and "Girl with the Dragon Tattoo."

Human evolution sometimes goes to extremes before it finds the middle road of healthy balance between male and female models. However, female machismo is not the answer.

SOCIETAL GENDER CORRUPTION

Historically in human evolution, there was a corruption of deep gender-essences, both male and female. Patriarchal society went to extremes in subjugating women's power. Women were socialized to be the proverbial doormats, subservient to men in the power hierarchy.

This perversion created an imbalance of love and power in the deranged male-model. Culturally, men became war-mongering barbarians, behaving badly. Women were subjugated under male domination.

Ancient wisdom says, "Men build the cities. Women bring the civilization." Without proper yin/yang energy balance, the culture goes akimbo. Today, both genders are out of balance, disowning their internal essence. Men need to claim their love. Women need to claim their power.

MATRIARCHY

Before patriarchy, in "pagan times," 25,000 BCE to 10,000 BCE, deities were feminine. Matriarchal societies were characterized by peace and equal distribution of labor. Matriarchies were not hierarchical or competitive. Rather, they emphasized co-creating as a team. They were relational, based on cooperation.

Matriarchal communities were tribal. Decisions were made in group circles rather than by corporate ladders and patriarchal hierarchy. Matriarchies were inclusive rather than exclusive.

MATRIARCHY'S ABUSE OF POWER

However, toward the end of matriarchal times, women abused their power over men. Women abused men in similar ways that women are currently oppressed, globally.

Today, the karmic debt of women has been repaid across thousands of years of patriarchal oppression of women.

PATRIARCHY

Patriarchy began approximately 10,000-8,000 BCE with Egyptian, Greek, and Roman times.

Almost four-thousand years ago, Abraham (1,800 BCE) laid the foundation for the three major patriarchal religions when he fathered Isaac and Ishmael. Through them, the three great monotheistic religions emerged: Judaism, Christianity, and Islam. Contemporary, patriarchal culture is shaped by these religions.

Historically, the writers of the *Torah* and the *Bible* were men. There is no word for goddess in these books due to gender prejudice in the writers. Also, archaeologists historically were men. They referred to the matriarchy as pagan, constructing a bias against women.

The word pagan was associated with female sexuality. Female sexuality was denigrated by patriarchal societies as profligate, excessive, out of control, and demented—leading to lawlessness, hysteria, and chaos. Much of the derangement in the world today is due to patriarchal gender confusion.

Look at the global, religious wars today involving the three patriarchal religions. **Abrahamic family wars embody quintessential family dysfunction through his sons Isaac and Ishmael. Isaac's progeny created Judaism and Christianity. Ishmael's offspring created Islam. Their sibling rivalry continues today** in the turf wars, power games, and tribal blood-feuds of the world's three great monotheistic religions.

This dysfunctional family on the global stage uses guns and bombs to express male action-derangement and abuse of power against women.

PATRIARCHY'S ABUSE OF POWER

In today's pivotal time of change, I'm reminded of Toni Morrison's poignant insight. She is one of the nation's greatest writers. As a senior woman of color, she has seen the unfolding of black men's identity and the patriarchal abuse of power.

She describes how in the 1950s, it was dangerous to be a black man. Black men were hung from trees in the South, "strange fruit" as the Billy Holiday song describes. Their homes were burned in the night. Black men and women, boys and girls were prohibited from white schools, shops, and easy travel. They were forbidden basic human rights, to vote freely, to use public restrooms, or to enter restaurants. As a black man, you could die or go to prison for a lifetime if you obeyed your instinctual code of manhood to stand for justice.

> **This is child abuse writ large by the patriarchal father figure, the government.**
>
> **Abuse of power is an action-derangement, a misuse of the male principle.**
>
> **It reflects a wounded male archetype in the culture.**

For abuse to exist, the male action-archetype is broken inside both men and women. After all, the people get the government that they elect.

WOMEN'S REVOLUTION OF THE 1960s

In the gender revolution of the 1960s, I witnessed a turning-point in the history of patriarchal abuse against women. I saw the invention of women's groups and group therapy at the grassroots level. Before that time, women were isolated.

Leaders of the women's movement like Betty Friedan and Gloria Steinem told women's stories. Women's groups arose in towns and cities across America. Having been muzzled for so long historically, women were desperate to speak—to each other, to the world, and to themselves.

Women healed themselves through talking. Communication unsealed the tomb of helplessness. Shared knowledge and information shined light on female oppression. Prior to that time, women were not conscious of their own stories. They had become numb to their victimization, normalizing it.

As they discussed their stories, women awakened to their lack of healthy, legitimate entitlement. From naming their experience and suffering, change could begin. Before that time, women didn't consciously claim ownership of their lives, let alone their entitlement.

Learning healthy boundaries and entitlement, women created a gender revolution. The price in pain was enormous. We do pay for our education. However, evolution will not be denied.

Fifty years later, women still only earn seventy-seven cents on a man's dollar for the same work. Although there is better work parity than the 1960s, women still have not penetrated the "glass ceiling" of executive management. In over two hundred years of the nation's history, we still have not seen a woman President, even though fifty-five percent of the population is female.

However, gender equality is better than it was. Women secured reproductive rights and birth control. They now have the right to work outside the home without social stigma. Today's women have property rights, the right to vote, and legal rights to their children.

There are visible women in government; anchor women appear on TV news; an increasing number of women own businesses; and over fifty percent of college graduates are female. There are more media scripts in films and television describing the women's journey than ever in history. There is some societal gender rectification.

THE PAINFUL PRICE OF PROGRESS

However, young people must not forget how recent these societal changes are and the terrible price in suffering that was paid for today's freedoms. These rights can easily be lost.

I have lived to see the changes. **My own grandmother did not have the legal right to her own children, to vote, to own property, to have a bank account, or to own the jewelry on her body.**

When I was growing up, there were no strong women in government or visible on the national stage, until Eleanor Roosevelt. There were no healthy women role-models in positions of power for a girl to emulate. The women's movement later coined the phrase "If you can't see it, you can't be it." Without role models, there was no path to power for women.

Women were infantilized, sexualized, or objectified as accessories to men's power. Listen to the unnaturally high-pitched, childish, kittenish voices of Marilyn Monroe and Jacqueline Kennedy to feel the insidious vacuum of healthy selfhood created by male oppression. These women were national icons—images that the nation revered! Watch the TV series "Mad Men" to catch a tiny glimpse of the oppression and injustice women suffered in the early twentieth century.

Women had no power in the society. There was no place for them in the marketplace. By contrast, a man was born with a birthright to the business world. Women were without access to money, except through a man.

No one validated a woman's power; rather, it was mocked and diminished, turned into a subversive perversion. Little girls were trained to submission, told they were "bossy" if they asserted themselves. In the same situation, little boys were told they had executive ability and leadership talent. These gender wars were a terrible loss of female leadership for the world.

Without independent identities, women lived to please men, to capture a husband, and to be "taken care of." The watchword for women was "don't make problems," "shut-up," "go along to get along." What a tragic burden for both genders to bear!

Look at the earlier film version of "The Stepford Wives" to see the calcified lock-down of women's lives. Not allowed careers, women were confined to the home, domestic duties, child raising, ladies' tea parties, and shopping. Other excursions were off-limits without a male escort. Sounds like the Taliban in today's world!

Domestic violence was legal in California and across the country until the 1970s. The term "domestic violence" was not invented until then. If a woman endured abuse in the home, her therapist quoted the *Bible* and said, "Women's place is to be subservient to men." She was at fault if her husband abused her. It was her job to try harder to please him.

In women's magazines, women were advised to spice-up their marriages by welcoming hubby home from work dressed in transparent Saran Wrap. Dinner must be hot and on the table at these pinnacle moments. Magical thinking and childish fantasies abounded in Lady-La-La-Land.

Clearly, we were not in the Land of Equal Co-Creation then. Nor, are we there yet.

MALE SHAME

At a subconscious level, men endure terrible guilt, shame, and pressure for their abuse of patriarchal power through recent millennia. This "human stain" is the same that women carried when they abused men through the matriarchy. Both genders suffer when the male action-principle is twisted.

Abuse of power splits a man from his manhood. To perpetrate injustice betrays his natural, male design which is to defend justice. When he abnegates his healthy instincts, it robs a man from himself. This is a tragic loss.

THE ABUSER'S PAIN

For men to reflect, to self-interview, and to own their part in subjugating women's power can advance both men and the culture. Importantly, men can name their own pain from being cast as the abuser, the tyrant, the egotistical power-monger in the Collective Play.

The abuser's wound is deep and profound. The abuser suffered tragically—usually in his family of origin, the culture, or past lives. The wound can be evasive to identify, such as abandonment, neglect, or lack of healthy models. How do you identify something that was not there?! Or, the wound can be more obvious from overtly aggressive, toxic parenting.

The abuser's pain from the injustice he suffered is disowned and projected onto others. In his internal scripts, the abuser often sees himself as a martyr being crucified by others—his spouse, the government, his boss, the law.

In an attempt to relieve his unconscious pain, the abuser misuses his power, targeting those under his control who are weaker—such as women, children, and employees. Abusers have unresolved issues around anger, control, and power.

Victims have the same issues, but in reverse. Victims typically internalize these issues, acting them inwardly in self-perpetration; while abusers act-out anger, control, and power issues. Victims often adopt a codependent role embodying covert, unaddressed, power issues.

Victims are passive; while abusers are active. Abusers can be overt ragers; victims can wield covert, passive-aggressive, toxic anger. Both are damaging.

Both abusers and victims can be unconscious offenders. They both engage in misplaced attempts to relieve their disowned suffering.

The abuser and the victim dance together, psychologically speaking. They are the front and the back of each other. You can't have one without the other. The victim and the abuser both arrive at the dance with a deranged male-archetype and unresolved action-issues.

MEN'S REDEMPTION

Each gender must redeem itself from sin. Men bear a terrible burden from the gender imbalance and abuse in the culture. The path to redemption is communication and open sharing. Naming the journey begins the healing.

Our men can make it safe to talk to each other about their deep feelings. Many men are not aware of their collective wound. They may be numb to their own stories, just as women were in the 1960s.

Male pain is locked inside because historically survival required a code of silence. A man on the frontlines of war, hunting for food, or defending his family from attack could not afford the luxury of self-exploration. He could jeopardize others if he spent energy hunting his wound in psychological inquiry. His full focus was required for survival.

Later, society taught him that his imperative was to earn a living. He had the burden of supporting a family. He had duties and responsibilities. It was easier to numb the pain by addiction, emotional avoidance, or work distraction.

Identifying and speaking of their pain could free men. Naming their experience without toxic shaming would go a long way.

Men empower themselves when they name their disowned shadow. They awaken from the societal hypnotic trance around abusive male power. Naming the abuser's suffering would help to lift the burden from men's shoulders and from their psyches.

However, men must remove the rock of oppression in their own way. Talking was the women's path to power. The men's path will involve more physical, kinetic, tribal ritual similar to Robert Bly's important work on men's consciousness. How men find the path through the complex jungle undergrowth of today's culture remains to be seen.

Stay tuned adventurers! Justice and balance can be redeemed. Men and women advance together in the yin-yang evolutionary climb.

HUNTING THE LIE

Meanwhile, with current male action-derangement, healthy selfhood is sacrificed on the altar of worldly achievement. The money-god prevails. Just where do we think we are going in our crazy-busy? What is this endless army of tasks that springs from the ground of dismembered being?

A societal lie remains—a big one. However, the Wheel always turns. Cosmic balance always wins.

To find the missing pieces in my personal search for healthy male and female, I hacked through a lot of personal jungle complexity. Jungians said, "As a woman, you must claim your healthy male." But what did that look like!? I had never seen a psychologically healthy man or woman.

In my struggle for wholeness, I took assertiveness training, PET (Parent Effectiveness Training), and conflict resolution classes. To regain my inner male, I claimed my "self-authority." I read all the psychology books on gender differences. I got a Ph. D. in Psychology for heaven's sake! I took the lead in business and defended my healthy entitlement. Yet, there still was something missing.

In my continued search for deep gender-essences, I explored esoteric gender models in Kabala and Native American Indian wisdom. The esoteric gender models turned my Wheel.

They ignited my deep dive into my personal internal gender-essence. These revelations shocked me. I uncovered my own original, mystical insights into gender essence.

In addition, I re-visioned some old *Bible* stories involving families— including Adam and Eve; as well as, Joseph and Mary.

ESOTERIC GENDER MODELS

In my ravenous search for deep gender-essence, I plumbed esoteric literature and lore. Esoteric wisdom often flips conventional wisdom on its head. Prepare for a flip!

DEEP GENDER-ESSENCE

In Western culture and Jung's archetypal psychology, mother is the symbol of unconditional love. Father is the symbol of power and authority. I discovered that these external, societal roles are the opposite of internal, deep gender-essences. Ha! What a surprise!

Esoteric gender models say yin and yang are only the external roles. The internal gender-essences are reversed. The deep female-essence is power, extreme yang. The internal male-essence is love, extreme yin. Who knew?!

> Internal gender-essences are the opposite of social roles.
>
> The internal essence of womanhood is power—extreme yang.
>
> The internal essence of manhood is love—extreme yin.

Because each internal gender-essence is extremely intense, it must be modulated by an opposite healthy, external social-role. Social roles balance and mitigate untrammeled, raw gender-essence, making it manageable. Social roles allow the person to carry his or her deep gender-essence with grace.

Healthy social-roles also provide equanimity allowing the society to function smoothly. They balance the culture and the individual energy.

Across millennia of society's gender abuse, the culture forgot about internal gender-essences. Today, we inherit that ignorance. In addition, instead of healthy social-roles to balance internal gender-essences, the culture presents each gender with a twisted, external role—men as barbarians, women as doormats.

> **Ignorance regarding internal gender-essence alienates you against yourself.**
>
> **It splits you inside.**
>
> **Society's twisted gender-role adds to the confusion.**

Deep inside your being, you know the truth of your internal gender-essence. It is crazy-making when society teaches you the opposite in social roles without anchoring you in your deep gender-essence. You can feel spun around, disoriented, and disconnected by societal gender lies. There is a feeling of betrayal by mentors who were supposed to guide you in wisdom training.

Now, instead of half-truths, I had discovered the entirety of my gender design.

DEEP FEMALE-ESSENCE

By contrast to social role, internal female-essence is raw, primal, creative power. It will not be denied. Think, "Hell hath no fury like a woman scorned." Deep female-essence is a force of nature, like a tornado or volcano. It is a dynamo that can easily be mismanaged.

Internal gender-essence finally explained the roar I heard inside! If I went around with my deep-roar running things, it would bite heads off. I understood why opposite social roles were necessary to balance raw essence.

My internal roar was naked power. It didn't feel personalized. It was more elemental, more primitive, more essential than the overlay of personality. It was a ruthless, survival life-force.

I knew that it could be destructive if unguarded. Deep female-essence definitely needed to be civilized. I could see how the external, submissive role of woman mitigated her untamed power, making it safe for everyone involved!

This internal female-essence is no sweet, love-goddess Venus. She is more like the ravenous Hindu goddess Kali whose "maw is dripping with blood" from recent devourings. Feral, ancient, ferocious, fierce, untamable are words that describe her. She is quite a shrew in her way. Sorry ladies. She certainly isn't what I had expected!

No wonder nature assigned women to labor in childbirth. Women's ferocious, internal strength could manage anything!

I also could see why the original matriarchy developed cooperative systems. They were essential to avoid women cannibalizing each other with their enormous power. Perhaps, because of women's internal essence of instinctual power, they understand more clearly than men how easily power can be abused. Power can quickly derail and go terribly awry. No wonder women became experts at relational rather than hierarchical power.

Women have a profound understanding of the dangers of power abuse, not only because they are tinier than men physically and easier targets of violence, but also because of their internal gender design.

This internal female-essence has a profound honesty. It is the same uncompromising, pure, naked truthfulness that I feel hiking in nature. In that regard, deep female-essence is supremely trustworthy. It has a kind of uncanny truth-telling that reads the mind of God.

I could see how the vibration of deep female-essence reformats as it moves up the God Ladder. In divine octaves, truth-telling manifests as conscience and the soul, Divine Mother.

DEEP MALE-ESSENCE

Male internal gender-essence is love. It is vulnerable, tender, soft, caring, sweet, sharing, and considerate. How complex men are beneath all the social roles! I saw how delicate men are inside. They are ultra-sensitive in their core design.

Maybe that's why men have historically had difficulty talking and owning emotions. A man could be easily overwhelmed because his emotions are so huge. Perhaps, intrinsic male sensitivity is the reason his ego must be protected, socially.

Male social-roles of leadership, authority, and power balance his innate sensitivity. Wielding power mitigates his deep delicacy. It shields his core nature, helping him to carry his deep gender-essence in a protected way.

There is an interesting addendum when I examined deep male-essence. With their high-powered testosterone, men are hard-wired for sex in a way that women are not. Men have sexual thoughts every seventeen seconds!

For healthy balance, men need women sexually. By accessing their deep design for love, men "capture" a woman's heart. In this regard, men's tender, deep-essence design helps them to satisfy their sexual drive.

A woman gives sex after she receives the man's love. The man gives love to receive sex. The heart and root chakras of the two designs once again balance on the Yin-Yang Wheel.

SOCIAL ROLES BALANCE GENDER ESSENCE

Esoteric wisdom says that social-roles are designed to balance the excess of each internal gender-essence. External roles compensate the internal energy so it doesn't overwhelm society or the individual. In the yin-yang of life, the energies integrate creating harmony.

With esoteric information, I felt redeemed. I no longer had to apologize for my roar! I was informed of its limits. In the Native American Indian tradition, they call it "**balancing your shields" when you keep your various levels of power organized in right order**.

I was finally able to balance my shields. After finding the source of my deep, inner roar, I made peace with external gender-roles. I humbly—and actually, rather gratefully—took up my female social-role as my shield.

The cover of my social role was a relief. It gave me healthy alternatives of loving, co-creating, and supporting to mitigate my internal power as a woman. Also, my social role connected me with the vibration of my soul, Divine Mother. I felt more complete.

FALSE SOCIAL TRAINING

We are living in what Hindus call the Kali Yuga, the darkest age of the greatest ignorance in human history. We live in a period of illusion and maya.

Deranged social models teach a man not to feel his emotions which are his deepest gift. Society de-legitimatizes man's intrinsic sensitivity. He's not given healthy coping skills to deal with his emotions. Instead, men are socialized to repress emotions, not to cry, to be self-centered, and to be aggressive. Often, the sports culture and entertainment media sell men a false image of manhood.

A distorted social-role shames the man against his deep gender-essence. It divides him against himself. Healthy social-roles would balance his sensitive, internal essence, not erase it. Healthy use of male power serves justice, rather than abuse.

We need to teach boys the difference between their external social-role and their internal essence. We can teach them to balance their internal love with the healthy use of their worldly power. The healthy male uses his manly power to protect the weak.

> **Rather than explain internal gender-essence to children, society ignores it.**
>
> **Rather than teach healthy social-roles, society presents twisted gender models.**

In a similar derangement of healthy social-roles, women are taught to be secondary and self-erasing. It is socially safe for a woman to cry, but unsafe to get angry or to lead. Healthy anger is the vital force defining healthy boundaries, personal space, and creativity.

Rather than balancing and legitimatizing a woman's deep power to create, she is estranged from it. Often, the glamour and media industries show women as sex objects. Unrealistic body images alienate women from themselves. Such superficial images trivialize women's true, internal power.

Each gender has lost touch with its deep, internal gender-essence. Twisted social-roles muzzle and stifle internal essence rather than stabilize it. Each gender feels split-off from itself.

Disconnection from gender essence and confusion regarding social role have warped our culture.

RECONNECTING GENDER-ESSENCE

Balance and integration are the keys to health for both genders. For a man to reconnect with his internal gender-essence, he must consciously develop love. The heart's wisdom balances his power role in society.

It is equally important for a woman to develop her power in the world, to balance her social training for love. Healthy use of female power reconnects her internal gender-essence.

To become whole, each gender must integrate both love and power. Both men and women need clear access to male and female principles—internally and socially. The Wisdom Way requires honest self-interview at each rung of the God Ladder.

JUNG REVISITED

Through esoteric wisdom, I had returned to my Jungian training. However, I was seeing it with new eyes. My discovery of internal gender-essence was more fundamental than the archetypal, behavioral overlay of gender roles. Jungian archetypes of animus and anima are behavioral patterns rather than primal, immutable, deep gender-essences.

Internal gender-essence is foundational and unchangeable. It doesn't develop across time as anima and animus do. Anima and animus mutate through the stages of life. By contrast, internal gender-essence is unchanging, source energy—a substrate beneath the roles and evolving masks of gender identity.

Internal gender-essence is perceived through instinctual awareness, not through the mind. This explains why I couldn't find it with my mind. Deep, internal gender-essence is sensed by direct-knowing.

Because it exists outside the mind's parameters, internal gender-essence is elusive to identify. Just as a fish doesn't perceive the surrounding water, deep gender-essence is so close that it's difficult to witness. It is so familiar that it becomes indistinguishable.

Internal gender-essence contrasts with the epiphenomenon of collective archetypes. Gender-essence is hard-wired into your core, deeper than roles, experiences, or identities. It is intrinsic and pervasive—an existential state of being. It is your organic design, inseparable from and inherent to your being human. Internal gender-essence is a constant across the field of your life.

FEMALE DEEP ROAR

My deep roar of power was not something that I could find outside me—in men, books, or classes. It was already inside me!

Gender-essence is like a constant engine, running night and day. It is inseparable from your being. It is not a spiritualized abstraction or learned behavior.

Internal female-essence is yang, including all the qualities that Taoists use to describe yang. It is primal energy, a force of nature.

Fathers and Fathering

It is a vital force for survival.

Female-essence has a profound instinct to separate lies from truth with ruthless radiance. Its truth-meter is uncanny and impeccable, because it is deeply aligned with the life force.

For conscious awakening, I simply had to witness and to acknowledge my internal gender-essence—my creative power as a woman—rather than erase and diminish it. Without realizing it, I had self-perpetrated. I had subtly colluded with society's erasure of my power as a woman. I had ignored my natural, inherent, deep gender-essence—my birthright of female power. I had not given my internal roar fair value.

The engine of female internal power is radically different from the external power of the male social-role. The two power engines are as different as the Hindu gods Kali and Shiva. Kali is depicted as red; Shiva as blue.

Kali's female power is direct and unyielding. She is an impersonal force of nature. She is radical, root power.

Kali is the primal energy of the Big Bang before it organized the cosmos into light and subsequently into matter. Kali is a creation goddess linking the Mind of God with the root-cause vibration of sound from which light and form later emerge. She predates Shiva, the creation god of manifest form.

Kali slaughters demons and illusions. Her necklace is made of human skulls. She triumphs over death and destruction by bringing rebirth.

Shiva is a softer energy than Kali; though both gods represent the Plutonian concept of creation and destruction. Through self-sacrifice, Shiva redeems humanity. His dancing image reflects his connection with the rhythms of the universe. He is definitely friendlier than Kali.

Frankly, both gender's power-engines can be severe and demanding. All power can be dangerous and easily abused. Power abuse can be external or internal; social or psychological. Both male social power and female internal power can become wild animals or tantrum-toddlers. All power requires civilizing and careful monitoring.

I could easily see why each gender needed the other and healthy social-roles for balance and taming so the culture would work smoothly. Both love and power, men and women are needed to complete the Yin-Yang Wheel.

But, how will the world find healthy, balanced, gender roles at this time of societal ignorance regarding internal gender-essence and twisted social-models?!

BALANCING YOUR SHIELDS

If you want to balance your shields, identify both your social role and your deep gender-essence. Take a fearless self-inventory, both of your outer role and your internal gender-essence.

Feel both the love and the power inside you. Assess how you wield your personal power and your love. Reference your parental models of how to be male and female. Who was more loving? Who was more powerful?

Witness how you use love and power throughout the day. Are love and power balanced in your life? Overview your yin and yang energies.

Are there recurring victim/tyrant scripts in your life? Do you bounce between self-loathing and grandiosity? Are you codependent or power-mongering? Overly submissive or too controlling? Are you lost in spiritual escapism or a Peter Pan in arrested development?

How do you feel around powerful people? Must you always win each argument? Or, can you surrender your ego and allow the other person to win? Do you feel grounded in your self-authority? Do you need outside approval for self-acceptance? Are you willful? Self-abnegating?

Do you schedule both relaxation and work; pleasure and discipline? Are you hyper-busy? Stressed? Pushing too hard? Do you schedule time to rest? Do you know how to both give and receive?

Any imbalance of yin or yang energy can signal a need for shield-adjustment.

LOVE/POWER INTEGRATION

Here are some suggestions for personal integration and healing. Feel the aliveness of your deep gender-essence—love or power—in your body and in your being. If you are a woman, hear the roar of your deep, internal female. If you are a man, feel the soft embrace of your safe-harbor, internal male.

Think of people who embody each deep gender-essence in your life, in history, literature, art, film and mythology. Which friends or family members embody healthy gender-essence?

Next, identify society's shadow projections on your external, gender social-role—women as helpless doormats, men as power-mongering barbarians. Think of people in history, literature, art, film, mythology, friends, and family who model these twisted societal roles. How would you adjust and correct each one? Re-design them. Play with alternative models of healthy social-roles.

Simply owning and energetically experiencing your internal gender-essence unleashes medicine to heal your social-role derangements. Validating your internal gender-essence sets your social role straight, so it doesn't feel unnatural. When you align with your core gender-essence, external roles move into harmony. You find a social role that complements and modulates your internal gender-essence.

Most people are unconscious of societal programming regarding gender. You reclaim lost power and love when you awaken from the hypnotic trance of collective beliefs. Delete false, negative, social projections on each gender. Have you been complicit in projecting twisted gender images—both male and female?

Healthy integration is also obscured by false programming from childhood models. Did your childhood training instill a bias toward or against your gender? Was your mother or father dominant or subservient? Do you feel hostile toward or envious of the opposite gender? Do you see your gender as damaged or inferior? Are your ideas about social roles frozen in twisted gender-models?

Regarding social roles, if you are a man, do you denigrate women in the culture? Do you expect women to serve you? Do you see women as sex objects for your pleasure? In a man-woman team, do you require superiority? How do you feel about a woman president?

If you are a woman, do you characterize men as pigs? Are you frightened if you are the only woman in a group of men? Do you feel the boss must be a man? Do you have both men and women friends? Would you vote for a woman president if she were qualified?

Regarding internal gender-essence, do you own and value your gender's deep-essence? If you are a man, can you experience yourself as loving and vulnerable? Do you regularly speak of your emotions? Do you own your feelings in an intimate relationship without embarrassment or defensiveness? Is it safe to cry? Do you practice listening with your heart?

If you are a woman, can you imagine yourself as head of a large corporation or in a leadership role? Do you defend your entitlement? Or, do you avoid healthy confrontation? Do you have power issues claiming either too much or too little credit? How do you deal with anger? Do you suppress or deny it? Or, do you honestly name and resolve it?

Disentangling from the jungle vines of societal and family hypnotic trances can be daunting. The society's gender-essence disconnect is disorienting. Twisted social-roles can be draining.

However, with integration, both genders can access healthy love and power; healthy self-mothering and self-fathering; leading and supporting.

SELF-PARENTING

As an adult, your job is to mother and father yourself. Accessing Divine Mother and Divine Father are essential to daily self-love and empowerment.

The ultimate use of power is loving service. By self-parenting, you demonstrate loving service to your inner child. For example, if the child needs either discipline or a hug, the healthy parent serves the child's needs in each moment.

Father as authority figure without love is tyrannical. Conversely, mother without disciplined boundaries is ungrounded and codependent.

Both the healthy mother and father archetypes are necessary for a healthy internal psychological family and for a healthy external family. Whether it's your roar or your safe-harbor that you are seeking, male-female wholeness is necessary for a happy life.

MY GENDER-ESSENCE JOURNEY

In my gender-discovery journey, I began by exploring **Taoist yin/yang energies which describe the duality in all earthly life and in male/female social roles.** Yin and yang, male/female, expand/contract, summer/winter, slow/fast, hot/cold—these polarized descriptions of energies help you to sort earthly experience. Yin and yang can be applied to describe anything in a dualized world.

I progressed to unwrap **Jungian archetypes which are behavioral roles** across cultures and time. The male/female archetypes of animus/anima evolve and develop as a person grows. They transform into a new image, reformatting as a new archetype. They morph. Jungian archetypes helped me to clarify male/female behaviors.

When I discovered esoteric, internal gender-essences, I realized that they are different from the Taoist gender social-roles and from the developmental models of Jung's anima and animus.

Deep gender-essence doesn't evolve or change across time. It's not an epiphenomenon, behavior, or social role. It is the bedrock of gender design.

Webster defines essence as "unchanging, foundational, intrinsic, elemental, permanent, as contrasted with variable phenomenal phases. It is indispensable to the nature of the thing."

While there are many applications of the word "essence," by discovering my internal gender-essence, I found a part of me that won't change between birth and death. I engaged with my intrinsic, foundational gender-self.

It relieved my nervous system to set things straight in my mind. Until then, I had unconsciously devalued and de-legitimatized aspects of myself. Unidentified, powerful forces inside me were confusing. Since my culture didn't validate my deep gender-essence, I had discredited an important part of myself.

Discovering my internal female-essence reinforced my natural entitlement, my right to exist. By re-claiming disowned energy, I took back my standing, self-authority, and dominion within myself. I could own clear self-assertion without hedging or compromising my power. I found my voice to say, "I want... I need...I feel..." The ontological guilt went away.

At first, realizing that the culture was ignorant regarding internal gender-essence shocked me. Gender is such an important element in the human journey.

Then, understanding society's blatant distortions of healthy social-roles saddened me. How could the collective be so lost in illusion?

My exploration of internal gender-essence didn't change the healthy aspects of gender social-roles. Rather, knowing my deep female-essence made it easier to embrace traditional, social gender-roles. I energetically understood the need for balance.

Discovering the hazards and limits of my internal gender-essence helped me to understand why society values gender social-roles so highly.

TRANSCENDING DUALITY

My Inner Guides continually reminded me to reference both my internal gender-essence of power and my female social-role of love in daily living. They said I must integrate the two, love and power, in order to balance my shields.

I must embrace both my male and female principles, both yin and yang, in the right application of each. Each occasion in the day demands a different male or female energy. Sometimes, my female essence of power is required. At other times, my social role of love is needed.

Knowledge of my internal gender-essence and healthy social-role expanded my freedom and awareness. Learning the limits of each gender allowed me to be of greater service to my partner, to myself, and to the world. Knowing the boundaries awakened me to healthy expectations.

Strangely, learning duality taught me the transcension of duality. Experiencing the limits of gender in a marriage partnership is an important tool in transcending the personal, earthly self into the divine realm.

On the journey to the Sacred Human, the ultimate task is to digest, assimilate, integrate, and transcend the earthly form—including both gender essence and social role. The many skills demanded in managing gender can provide some dominion on the Sacred Path.

Today in society, as the genders retool, we must increasingly honor the Divine Feminine to restore balance. Soul installation is essential for humans to evolve. Soul embodiment must return to earth. Healthy limits and conscience can remedy male action-derangement. Divine Mother's nurturing can make it safe for all of us.

In addition to the Divine Feminine, the Divine Masculine is also needed. Divine Masculine sustains and protects rather than the shadow male who dominates and destroys. Divine Masculine transcends ego rather than abusing personal power. He brings justice, truth, and divine law.

Knowledge of the Divine Feminine and the Divine Masculine in the culture requires awakening. Male/female energies traveling the Sacred Path in co-creation evolves the Sacred Human so needed to solve the complex problems in today's world.

MY GENDER CONCLUSIONS

Through my deep-dive into gender, I saw the need for balancing love and power in the public arena. I saw how twisted social-roles have become with recent cycles of patriarchal abuse.

I realized that for society to evolve and for healthy parenting to prevail, going forward involves:

1. Education regarding internal gender-essences—their relative gifts and hazards. Teaching how to balance gender-essences with healthy social-roles.

2. Redefining gender social-roles. Encouraging both genders to develop love and power. Teaching the right use of both love and power. Helping both genders to learn leadership,

as well as support skills in social-roles.

3. Repairing the broken male-principle in the culture. Correcting action addiction, abuse of women, devaluation of yin energy, and money-god fixation.

4. Developing a relationship with the Sacred Feminine—the soul—the nurturing Divine Mother. Remedying the loss of conscience and healthy limits through soul embodiment. Anchoring the soul energetically in the body, so the Divine Mother is not a remote, mental abstraction.

5. Developing a conscious relationship with the Sacred Masculine—the spirit—Divine Father who values ego transcension and selfless service for the good of the whole. Consciously embodying spirit.

6. Teaching the lived-experience of the energy differences between Divine Mother and Divine Father.

7. Evolving the Wise Man, the Wise Woman, and the Path of Wisdom.

Healthy parenting requires expanding beyond personal ego. When we integrate and transcend the personal, we move into wisdom worlds. My excursions into esoteric wisdom gave me profound respect for spiritual intelligence.

To survive in the Human Experiment, we need wisdom technologies to manage complex personal and global problems. Healthy families are a key to teaching and learning wisdom. From healthy parenting, the Wise Man and the Wise Woman can be born.

KABALA GENDER MODELS

To further enrich my understanding of deep gender-essence, I studied Kabala, the Jewish mystical tradition. In contrast to Western psychological and cultural stereotypes of male and female, Kabala presents the gender journey in the three pillars of the Tree of Life. On the left is the female pillar, called "severity". On the right is the male pillar, called "mercy".

The center pillar is equilibrium, the balance and integration of both the male and female principles. In the middle, you become an empty, pure channel for God. Your chakras are clear of illusions that distort reality. You are an instrument for good in the world. Goodness is the joining of love and truth, male and female.

Through the clear channeling of the central-pillar, each gender serves the other. Each gender delivers both love and power to the other and to itself.

In Kabala, the reason woman is called severity is related to Saturn, the form-giver. Saturn defines the laws or limits of the kingdom. Saturn is the archetype of authority—the limit-setter for earthly boundaries.

Woman is the truth-teller and the form-giver. In giving birth she gives shape to life. She contains the life-giving spirit of sperm, gestating it into human form. Woman is the vessel that channels spirit down the God Ladder onto earth.

In my personal journey through Kabala, I could understand the woman as form-giver, setting limits, and thus representing severity. After all, it is the woman who must say "No" in sex, according to her menstrual cycle and courtship requirements. She is the gatekeeper to her body.

However, I couldn't grasp the male principle as mercy until I spoke with Joseph, the father of Jesus.

JOSEPH, FATHER OF THE HOLY FAMILY

To further understand fathering and deep male-essence, I meditated with the holy father, Joseph. I was disconcerted by all the societal attention that went to Mary, the holy mother. The father principle in Joseph seemed neglected. In the interest of gender parity, for a year I meditated for one hour a day, five days a week with Joseph. His wisdom touched me deeply.

MY JOSEPH JOURNEY

In meditation, Joseph revealed his internal gender-essence. He said his deep nature as a man is mercy. At first, I didn't understand what he meant. Though I had studied Kabala and esoteric models, I was still immersed in Western cultural images of the powerful male and the submissive female.

Joseph said,

> *Come with me to my tiny hometown in ancient Judea. Keep in mind, there are strict laws of behavior for betrothal. Only virgins are honored in marriage.*

Imagine what I go through when my betrothed, Mary, shows up pregnant! Then, she asks me to believe that it is an immaculate conception!!

We lived in a closed society where unmarried pregnant women were shunned—even banished for life or stoned to death. Being betrothed to pregnant Mary put both our lives at risk.

When she announced her pregnancy as a virgin, I was enraged. She had betrayed me. I was furious. How could she do this to me!? Then, I was depressed. I was so caught-up in myself, I couldn't see anything else. Days went by.

Mary talked about an angel. She cried. She begged me to believe her. She kept repeating that her baby was not conceived by a man. She was a virgin. Imagine if your beloved told you this preposterous story!

The psychological and spiritual journey Joseph travelled to arrive at love was extraordinary. To continue loving Mary, Joseph was asked to move beyond his own ego. He must surrender his rational mind to accept Mary's crazy story. He must love her more than he hated her story.

In addition, Joseph had to surrender his self-image in the community. He risked tragic isolation, shame, and disapproval.

He was asked to accept to a larger will than his own, God's will. To get there, somehow, he had to listen to the deeper, inner voice of his soul—his Divine Feminine.

JOSEPH'S JOURNEY

To find love, Joseph's soul told him

Dear One,

To honor God's will, you must find mercy and forgiveness for Mary. You must move into selfless surrender. Think of how God loves you—unconditionally—beyond your behavior of right and wrong. God redeems you every time you fall from grace. Find that unconditional love inside you.

I am here. I will guide you every step of the way, one stepping-stone at a time. I will lead you. Just listen to my voice inside you.

To love Mary, Joseph had to forgive the possibility that the child was conceived by another man. This mercy and forgiveness were totally foreign to his life as a man. In his time and culture, *lex talionis*—an-eye-for-an-eye—and revenge were the mode.

Joseph had to transcend his childhood training, his culture, and his own ego to love Mary. He had to by-pass his personal, earthly world. He even had to drop his mind to transcend into the irrational place of loving.

By dropping his left-brain, critical "monkey-mind," Joseph discovered deeper love. He found his manly deep-essence to protect, nurture, defend, and even to die for his beloved. He found true love.

Joseph's personal identity had to die so he could transcend into serving God. Then, he could embrace unconditional love.

JOSEPH'S AGONY

Trying to resolve his inner conflict, Joseph experienced great agony. He compared it to Mary's subsequent agony at the crucifixion.

At the cross, Mary sacrificed her greatest treasure to God. She gave her beloved son to die as a criminal. Out of love for God and respect for God's will, Mary surrendered her personal will.

"Thy will be done" was more than a *Bible* quote for both Mary and Joseph. They both humbly bent the knee to God's unfathomable, transcendent will—God's Great Mystery.

Mary and Joseph trusted God's plan beyond their own. In serving God, they transcended the limits of earthly duality.

MARY'S AGONY

Michelangelo's extraordinary sculpture, the Pieta, accurately depicts Mary's agony—her surrender and sacrifice. With her dead son lying broken and limp across her lap, she extends her hands to God. She brings her greatest gift to God. On the altar of sacrifice, she surrenders her son in service to God's inscrutable will.

Mary's extended arms form a cross against her vertical body. Her ego is crucified with her surrender. She honors God's will, even though it is the opposite her own. Mary respects God's vision as greater than her own. She trusts God, beyond herself.

Mary and Joseph's selfless sacrifice allows the greatest miracle in human history, the miracle of Christ's resurrection from the dead, demonstrating life beyond death. The holy family's ego-surrender serves the entire family of humanity.

JOSEPH'S SURRENDER

When he accepts his betrothed—a pregnant virgin—in marriage, Joseph surrenders his mind on the altar of sacrifice. He moves beyond his social role into his deep male-essence of mercy, forgiveness, and love. This is his ego crucifixion.

Joseph demonstrates the internal male-essence when he forgives Mary. Love is an irrational act that is often counter-logical and beyond the mind.

By connecting with his internal love-essence, Joseph activates his divine self. He listens to God's voice rather than his personal scripts. He honored God's will over his personal desire. He loves God more than his pictures of how life should be.

God gave Joseph a difficult Soul Contract. Maybe you don't have a partner with an immaculate conception. Maybe you haven't been tested as Joseph was. However, you still must transcend yourself to find love. Love is a leap of faith. It is a sacrificial act that often requires crucifying the personal ego.

Mary asks Joseph to transcend reason, to drop his mind. She asks Joseph to forgive and to move beyond his selfish ego. Mary invites Joseph to join her in the realm of spirit.

All women invite men into the same dance. Through love, each gender transcends into divine realms.

SACRIFICE

Healthy sacrifice can magically transmute negative to positive energy. When we reunite with our divine, transcendent nature, we consecrate earthly life. Sacrifice is sacramental. It makes earthly life sacred.

Man's approach to life is left-brain, rational, and goal-oriented. Woman's approach is right-brain, irrational, intuitive, oceanic, not only connected with reason—but with divine realms beyond duality.

The great Sufi poet Rumi says

> *Out beyond right and wrong*
> *There is a field.*
> *I'll meet you there.*

Out beyond earthly duality, that's where love lives.

To obey God's will and marry pregnant Mary, Joseph had to sacrifice his worldly view, his rational approach, and his limited, earthly self. To honor Mary in love, Joseph transcends himself. He reaches love through sacrifice.

JOSEPH'S MERCY

Joseph's deep gender-essence is loving mercy. Mercy can only be wielded by those who have strength and power. Mercy is an irrational act. It opens the door to love, forgiveness, and healing.

Mercy transcends the rational mind. Forgiveness is connected with faith. Every father follows Joseph's path.

For men to balance love and power in service to the Great Mystery is the spiritual path. Family life teaches fathers self-transcension, love, and mercy—the right use of power.

You don't have to be a father to have the experience of fathering. You administer fathering whenever you are merciful, forgiving, loving, protective, safe, and selfless. Everyone self-parents their inner selves throughout each day.

Call upon Joseph. Think of the immensity of his journey into love. Joseph will help you to develop your healthy, internal male. He will guide you in fathering.

TRANSCENDING SOCIAL ROLES

Transcending the small self feels unnatural at first. Transcending old, familiar habits and identities can be terrifying.

However, transcending the old is the path to the new. Both genders can calcify inside their social roles. If you don't grow, you are jailed in the frozen past.

Joseph's courage to explore his deep male-essence of mercy freed him from societal confines. He then could be of greater service to the Divine Plan.

MARY'S POWER

Think of Mary's journey to her deep female-essence and owning her power. She risked everything when she told Joseph the truth of her virgin pregnancy. She came out of hiding. It was a counter-intuitive, counter-culture act.

To language her journey to Joseph, Mary had to find her deep, internal, creative power to act. Mary's speaking the unspeakable required enormous inner strength. She risked death if he rejected her. She could have been stoned or banished for life.

Both Mary and Joseph traversed the many worlds to find the love and the power to serve God. To be human is a heroic bridging of the worlds—earthly and divine; male and female.

In the human journey, the earthly and the divine worlds marry. As parents of the holy family, Mary and Joseph are way-showers for all of us—mothers and fathers, men and women.

SKY FATHER AND EARTH MOTHER

THE DIVINE ENERGY SPECTRUM

To deepen my understanding of gender, I studied for sixteen years with various shaman. I uncovered esoteric Native American Indian wisdom.

It teaches that Sky Father and Earth Mother are nature's presentation of the male and female principles. Spirit and matter need each other to create human life. In this gender model, Sky Father represents male, spirit. Mother Earth represents female, matter.

Male and female culminate at opposite ends of the energy spectrum or God Ladder. Deep male-energy is extreme yin. It is expanded love energy which ultimately becomes spirit in Sky Father.

Deep female-energy is extreme yang. Her energy is power or creative potential—the power to give birth. A woman's yang energy is so compacted that it manifests in dense, physical form as a baby. Woman's extreme yang becomes matter, Earth Mother.

On the journey into human form, Divine Spirit, Sky Father moves down the God Ladder into matter. He uses Earth Mother's components for physical embodiment. Our flesh and blood come from Earth Mother's elements.

Remember, the Yin-Yang Wheel turns and flips when the extremes overload. On the energy spectrum, during the descent into matter, extreme divine, yin spirit contracts so much that it transforms into earthly, yang matter. Matter is a condensed form of spirit.

Earthly life is a heavy format of gravity-entrapped Divine Light. You might say that expansive, free, divine spirit is imprisoned in inert, limited, earthly matter.

On the reverse journey to divine reunion at death, the male/female energies of spirit and matter flip again. In their dynamic dance, the extreme yang energy of earthly matter expands to become extreme yin, divine spirit. The divine spirit trapped in matter returns up the God Ladder. Spirit is released from matter, completing the journey home—free at last.

MALE/FEMALE: SPIRIT AND MATTER

Both the male and female energies are needed for balance in the earth walk. Woman's power is the contracted, yang format of spirit. Man's spirit is the expanded, yin format of matter. Both yin and yang exist within each gender. However, the opposite gender spark is needed to activate the deep, internal gender-essence.

The woman cannot create life without the life-giving sperm. Spirit is infused into flesh by God and by man, to enliven form. Earthly flesh is dead without the yin, male spirit.

Conversely, to be whole, the man's spirit needs the information stored in matter. He receives this "education" through the woman. She activates, anchors, and integrates his gender-essence, spirit on earth.

Without the form-giving component of matter, spirit dissipates and scatters. Male spirit needs female matter to focus it. She helps his spirit to descend the God Ladder into manifest form. The form-giving female contains the expansive male energy.

Similarly, female earth needs male spirit to awaken her core gender-essence, lifting it up the God Ladder. The woman's power requires the spiritual alignment and attunement that activate through the man. Matter without spirit is inert and lifeless. The male energy enlivens the female's creative power.

The male and female principles are essential to human life. Sky Father and Earth Mother marry in the human experience.

- In creating life, man activates the woman's inherent form-giving power. The woman's body then channels spirit and sperm into matter creating birth.
- The woman contains the man's spirit so it is not lost. Man needs woman to focus and direct his nature. He needs her to learn earth's secrets.
- Woman needs man to activate and inspire her nature. He is an agent aligning the evolution of her spirit.
- Man offers spirit. Woman offers form-giving matter.
- Woman conveys spirit into matter, moving spirit down the God Ladder into earthly form.

HEAVEN AND EARTH MARRY

Human life is the marriage of heaven and earth. Spiritual growth brings conscious awareness of spirit and matter, male and female, love and power, Sky Father and Earth Mother.

Purifying your consciousness and awakening awareness clarifies your experience of Sky Father and Earth Mother as they marry in your body each day. The child they parent is your earthly life.

Every inhale brings Sky Father down through your crown chakra to infuse your body with renewed spirit. Every exhale brings Earth Mother up your body through your feet, grounding and integrating spirit in matter. Your exhale informs God of the human experience.

Through you, the Divine Union of male and female naturally occurs. By the marriage of Sky Father and Earth Mother in you, the genders dialogue in the evolutionary journey up the God Ladder.

Judith Larkin Reno

INDIAN WEDDING BLANKET

The Native American Indian tradition honors the core gender-essences of male and female, spirit and matter, love and power. In her iconic painting "Crow Blanket," Penni Anne Cross portrays the gender energy-exchange. The bride and groom spread their multi-colored wedding blanket across the dark, desert floor on their wedding night.

The woman in her white deerskin wedding dress stands contrasted like a tower of light against the black night sky. A mighty fortress of strength, she plugs directly into infinite spirit, Sky Father above her head.

The groom is at her feet on the wedding blanket, holding her hand in love and adoration. He calls to her. She listens to him.

His willingness to be humble and loving enlivens her deep gender-essence of creative power. She channels Sky Father, bringing Great

Spirit to earth to serve him.

Thereby, she activates his core energy. She opens him to receive his birthright, his inherent gender-essence—love which expands into spirit and Sky Father. Through his initial sexual motivation, he receives much more. His bride delivers abundant, divine dispensation.

Together, they potentiate each other, flowing in the Yin-Yang Wheel of Life. They both receive God through the profound gifts of gender—love and power, spirit and matter.

WOMEN'S POWER/MAN'S LOVE

In the Native tradition, the woman's creative power is deeply respected. Woman's blood is considered sacred. It carries the power to create babies. She is honored as the pleuripotent, creative life-force, Earth Mother. The woman contains the mysteries of life.

The man needs the woman to access Great Spirit on earth. A woman opens the path to God for a man. By connecting him to spirit, she catalyzes and empowers his core gender-essence of love, expanding it into spirit.

Man is already anchored on earth by his physical weight and size. His superior strength is needed to protect and defend the tribe. His deeper task is to elevate—to reunite with God, spirit, his gender-essence of love. Through personal, human love, he transcends to divine, universal love.

Woman does not need the man to access God. By her design, she can directly channel spirit. She needs man for protection. He also helps her to stay humble in the face of her great creative power, so she doesn't become grandiose and "play God." Anchored by his love, man guides woman to carry her power in a balanced way.

Also, the woman needs a place to put her creative power. The man focuses her power, helping the woman to evolve through service. Without focus, she could explode with too much power moving chaotically in every direction. Or, her power could implode inwardly creating depression.

Hard-wired inside every woman, there is a relationship manual full of her creative powers. Women are born fixer-uppers. They are constantly improving their homes, wardrobes, friends, children, and mates.

The man needs a place to put his enormous sex drive, designed to perpetuate the species. By loving a woman, he ultimately discovers his inherent, spiritual nature.

Each gender balances the other. The Native chiefs are all married. They understand that they access Great Spirit through the woman's power. The woman "balances the man's shields" and vice versa.

In the life of the tribe, the grandmother is the highest power. The chief must listen and honor her voice.

WOMEN'S BLOOD

The woman's creative power is closely connected with her blood. Her menstrual blood is placed on the crops to help them grow, reproduce, and bring a full harvest. Woman's blood literally contains the divine mysteries of life-giving power.

A man accesses this power through his woman. To complete his initiation into manhood, young men are expected to find a bride and to marry.

In their monthly cycle, when women bleed, they cleanse the entire tribe of its negativity and mistakes. At the time of menstruation, women are at their most powerful, extreme yang. Through their monthly empowerment, women literally purify the tribe and make it whole. A man's life is renewed each month through his woman's gift.

Fathers teach their sons to revere and to respect women's power as a gateway to Great Spirit. Through the marriage bond, a man receives his full manhood, his complete empowerment of spirit, each month.

When a woman ages, she no longer menstruates. Instead of babies, she turns her blood into wisdom. The Wise Bloods are the most revered in the tribe. The grandmothers are more powerful than the chief.

For more information on women's blood mysteries, see Roberta Cantow's wonderful film: *Bloodtime, Moon Time, Dream Time*. You can find it at www.originaldigital.net.

INDIAN MOON LODGE

When women live together in a tribal way, they bleed together—

usually at the new or full moon. Each month, the women gather in the Moon Lodge during their periods. While there, the women rest and renew.

They tell each other stories of the past month. The women heal themselves by talking and laughing together. If one woman experiences a tragedy, they all share wisdom to heal her. The sharing of community lifts each woman's burden. She is no longer alone.

The Wise Bloods are particularly revered in the Moon Lodge. Grandmothers carry the greatest wisdom both in the Moon Lodge and in the tribe. The young women look up to them as models of strength and deep-knowing. In tribal culture, wisdom only comes with age.

The fathers teach their sons to value the women's monthly cycle. They teach the boys to honor the great service that women provide to the tribe by cleansing and renewing them. The boys learn to value woman's power to create life and to give birth. The males revere the female blood mysteries.

During the Moon Lodge, the men and boys cook and clean the women's homes. They prepare food for each meal, bringing it to the Moon Lodge. They set the food outside the door for the women to eat. The men consider it an honor and a privilege to serve the women. Loving service returns the men to their core male-essence.

The transmutative power of the women's communal sharing renews the entire tribe. Everyone is made whole. Together, they are ready to face the month ahead.

THE LIGHTNING YEARS

Contrary to the ageism of Western culture, Native American Indian elders are esteemed. During tribal gatherings, the elders are honored. They stand in the center of the tribal circle.

The entire tribe acknowledges the elders for having seen the most lightning and lived to tell about it. Their long survival requires skill and Great Spirit's blessing. Their senior wisdom is seen as a gift to the entire tribe.

Wisdom only comes through passing many seasons. Wisdom is revered as the highest value of the tribe. I talk more about this in my book ***The Lightening Years: Menopause as Spiritual Initiation.*** In this title, there is a lightning-bolt graphic drawn through the –e in Lightening. The book moves through the beautiful bleeding years into the Wise Blood years, further illuminating the woman's wisdom journey.

THE FIRST FATHER'S DAY

To gain richer insight into deep gender-essences and fathering, imagine the First Father's Day. Travel back in time to the first couple. Adam and Eve are frolicking in the Garden of Eden, unencumbered by babies.

They are happy in their innocence. Swinging across the jungle canopy, they hunt and forage for food together. There is no division of labor or separation of roles.

They are equals. They are in primal union—prior to separation into duality consciousness.

The plot thickens when Eve gets pregnant. Adam and Eve are innocent. They have not yet awakened to knowledge of duality and gender differences. They don't know that babies come from sexual intercourse.

As her body changes shape, Eve is not as efficient at hunting and foraging as she once was. She can no longer be Adam's equal in food gathering. Adam carries an increasing burden in the partnership.

The day the baby drops out of woman's body, everything radically changes. The fall from grace begins.

THE FALL FROM GRACE

Now, imagine you are a man in today's world. You're playing basketball with a bunch of male buddies. Every Saturday for years, you've played basketball together. There's jovial ribbing, joking, and even a few pranks. Over the past weeks you've noticed one of your buddies has gained some weight. You don't think anything of it.

Suddenly, one day during a practice game, a baby drops out of your buddy's body! Imagine the other men's emotional and psychological experience of that.

Imagine the shock! A veil falls between the baby-creator and the other men. The men are no longer the same buddies as before the birth.

This fall from the grace of unity is similar to Adam's experience of Eve on the First Father's Day. This veil of separation is the original sin.

ADAM'S FATHER'S DAY

When Adam first sees the tiny baby emerge from Eve's body, he doesn't know what it is. He has never seen a human baby. It is a foreign and fascinating creature.

Adam picks the baby up and carefully examines it. His awe and wonder intensify. What is this strange being?

The baby arouses deep recognition in Adam. Their faces are similar. They both have two hands and feet, with ten fingers and toes. The baby cries with a high-pitch, tiny voice that Adam has never heard—yet it is not unlike his own yelps and screams. Wow! Adam is hypnotized in wonderment.

Suddenly, he steps back. Adam is shocked and amazed by Eve's power to give birth. He thinks, "If she can create a baby, she has power over life. If she has power over life, she has power over death. If she has power over life and death, she has power over me!"

Adam feels profound fear of Eve's enormous power. The fear is in his gut. It is instinctual fear for his survival.

But there's more. Adam also feels jealous of Eve's power. After all, a baby has never dropped out of his body! Why not?! Adam is envious. He has never experienced jealousy.

And, for the first time, Adam feels self-doubt. Where is his power? Is he not as powerful as Eve?!

He becomes conscious of himself as separate from Eve. Before the baby, they were united in an ocean of unconscious play. Now, he is seeing her with new eyes. A veil of separation has fallen between the two of them.

When they've hunted and foraged for food in the past, it was a game. He felt fun, focus, and necessity. No egos were involved. It was just "Go! Get food!"—a game, plain and simple.

Now, Eve has brought all this new complexity into Adam's life. He is discovering his emotional body in a way that he never knew before. And, these emotions hurt. Adam thinks "Eve is hurting me." "She is not safe." "She is the enemy."

Where did these unruly emotions come from? Before the baby, there was no duality. There was only unity. Now, there is separation. He thinks, "It's all her fault!"

THE ORIGINAL SIN

When you tune into Adam's jealousy and follow it back to its origin, you feel his awe and wonder at Eve's power. He thinks, "I couldn't do that!"

He also feels separation. "She has power that I don't have."

Adam's feelings are mixed and jumbled. He feels protective of the baby, fascinated by this tiny, sweet, new life. However, he also feels burdened having yet another mouth to feed!

Now, Adam must hunt and gather food for three people rather than just one. His labor has considerably multiplied—all because of Eve.

For the first time, Adam feels separate from Eve. **This separation is the original sin.**

EVE'S MOTHER'S DAY

Meanwhile, Eve is amazed at her power to give birth. It is a miracle. To see another human life emerge from your body is awesome and wondrous.

However, as time goes by, she sees the veil of separation in Adam's eyes. What is it? Is it suspicion? Fear? Mistrust? After all these years as best friends, how could he mistrust her?

Eve thinks that the block between them must be because of her. It's clear that before the baby, Adam and Eve were close. After the baby, there is a separation. The baby did come out of her body.

Eve figures that she must be to blame for the separation. She must have done something wrong. She feels guilty for her unbidden power to give birth.

> **Separation between Adam and Eve is the fall from grace.**
>
> **Loss of unity consciousness is the original sin.**
>
> **The First Father's Day brings the first sin.**

SIN IS SEPARATION

When the veil of separation falls for Adam, it falls for all humanity. Separation consciousness is the opposite of divine unity consciousness.

One definition of sin is separation. Separation consciousness creates hierarchy, blaming, oppression, power games, and abuse. Separation leads to better-than or less-than thinking.

It turns your partner from a human into an object. Separation consciousness is at the root of tyrant/martyr and victim/perpetrator behavior. Polarized, oppositional thinking is the essence of war. It is a hazard of living on the earthly plane of duality.

Separation consciousness is a form of ignorance. In separation consciousness, you are entranced by earthly events (matter) at the expense of God union (spirit). You only inhabit the lower rungs of your God Ladder, your earthly nature, without accessing your entirety, including your divine nature.

EARTHLY DUALITY

God places Adam and Eve on earth, where they are immersed in a realm of duality and separation. God's learning agenda for Adam and Eve involves their conscious awakening to both earthly and divine worlds in the human experience.

Earthly life is characterized by opposites: male/female; yours/mine; up/down; left/right; hot/cold; summer/winter; pleasure/pain; war/peace. By definition, polarized earthly reality creates separation.

Duality is the way it is here on earth. It comes with your birth certificate. The moment you experience earthly duality, you know separation, whether you are conscious of it or not. You are separated from your Divine Source, your oneness.

However, when you enter flesh, you still retain far-memory of your Divine Home. Divine Union is encoded in your DNA. Because you are immersed in doo-doo duality, doesn't mean that you forget your divine nature. It haunts you!

You feel as if a piece of your puzzle is missing until you awaken to remember your divine nature. Over time, you realize that both natures are needed in the human journey—your earthly duality and your divine oneness.

Everyone who enters flesh receives an introduction to sin. The Garden of Eden story describes the descent down the God Ladder from the divine world of spirit into earthly matter. The moment there is separation consciousness, you have fallen from the grace of unitive, divine consciousness.

The trick is to awaken from the earthly trance and remember your divine oneness. God's invitation is to carry both your earthly and divine natures with integrity while you are in flesh.

DIVINE UNITY

Before awareness of duality, Adam and Eve live in a perfect Garden of Eden. Once separation begins, they descend the God Ladder into earthly, dualized consciousness.

By contrast to duality, divine consciousness is not aware of differences. It is absorbed in the oceanic bliss of being. All is one. There is no duality, opposition, or conflict. There is no subject-object awareness. There is no other, no you/me. There is only us. We are one.

Unity consciousness resides in your upper four chakras at the upper four rungs of your God Ladder: intuition, soul, spirit, and Universal God Source. They represent your divine nature.

Before you enter earthly duality, you are immersed in divine worlds. The poet Wordsworth says, "Birth is but a sleep and a forgetting." We all come "trailing clouds of glory," straight from God, before "shades of the prison-house begin to fall."

Awakening from doo-doo duality is not always easy. The earthly trance is compelling. The material girl is not necessarily Lady Ga-Ga for God. Remembering your divine nature can be rigorous—especially when your earthly nature blocks the way.

Your earthly nature includes your physical body, your emotions, and your mind. They can be a mine-field of messy complexity to transcend. These lower rungs on the God Ladder are heavy vibrations filled with illusions that are difficult to penetrate.

You see the rigors that Adam and Eve face in their heroic journey to love and service through family life. Their internal struggle between unity and duality, good and evil, earthly and divine worlds is a morality play writ large.

The beauty of being human is that you can access both your earthly and divine natures. But, how do you resolve your opposite natures—earthly and divine—when they are at war? How do you grow large enough to embrace them both? How do you co-create with battling factions of yours and mine, male and female in the world?

Adam and Eve wrestle with these important questions in the Garden of Eden.

THE LOSS OF DIVINE UNION

On the First Father's Day, for the first time Adam sees the difference between himself and Eve. The original sin is perceiving duality. The knowledge of good and evil is the awareness of separation—at the expense of God union.

With this conscious awakening, Adam and Eve cover their nakedness, feeling guilty for their gender differences. Prior to the fall from grace, there was a child-like innocence protecting both Adam and Eve.

Expulsion from the Garden of Eden comes when unity consciousness stops. Adam's fear and jealousy of Eve's creative power brings the first separation.

> **Man's fear of woman's creative power is the original sin.**

Perhaps, this fear of women's power is why early patriarchal writers of the *Torah* and the *Bible* described the original sin as belonging to Eve. They projected their disowned shadow onto the female.

When Eve accepts Adam's projection of fear rather than transmuting it, she colludes in his sin. She forgets her divine nature. She self-abandons and splits against herself. She lives Adam's life better than her own. Accepting his lie, she feels ashamed of her innate, deep, female power.

Today, we are still suffering from the legacy of Adam and Eve's gender war. To return to unity consciousness, both men and women must forgive women's power. Women must make it safe to be powerful—both for themselves and for men.

REDEMPTION THROUGH FAMILY

On the First Father's Day, despite his fear, self-doubt, and jealousy, Adam gets food for Eve and the baby. Instead of running away, he stands and serves his family. He protects them.

The only reason Adam stays is love. Adam serves Eve and the baby out of mercy and selflessness. He transcends his ego. There is nothing in the arrangement for Adam—except love.

Adam could feed himself alone. He could allow Eve and the baby to die. Instead, parenting returns Adam to his deep gender-essence as a man, which is selfless service in love.

When he gets food for his new family, Adam transmutes humiliation into humility. He moves from power games into God union. As he embraces his deep male-essence, he claims his complete God Ladder and his divine inheritance. Loving service is the highest power and the deepest privilege on earth.

> **Through serving his family, Adam heals the original sin of separation.**

Through Adam's love, mercy, and forgiveness, Eve is able to forgive herself for her creative power. She returns to God union and her deep female-essence. Both Adam and Eve receive redemption through family life.

Adam's humble service in the face of Eve's power allows her to return his love. And, his love allows her to be powerful.

By parenting, Adam transcends gender separation. He leads humanity to God union as he heals the original sin of separation. Through family, together Adam and Eve redeem women, men, and humanity.

CONSCIENCE

Adam's knowledge of good and evil through Eve teaches him

morality. It awakens his conscience, his soul. Adam serves Eve and the baby despite his fear. By listening to his Divine Feminine, he transcends his limited earthly self. By obeying, the first man anchors his soul on earth.

Through love, Adam brings Divine Mother to earth in humanity's first soul embodiment. On the First Father's Day, when Adam moves up his God Ladder to embrace his soul, he becomes an agent of God's divine plan.

> **On the First Father's day, Adam activates humanity's first soul embodiment.**

LOVE

Love is the unifying force that unlocks the duality bind. Selfless service reunites Adam and Eve with their divine birthright. Oneness remedies the sin of separation and restores their divine nature.

Eve receives Divine Father, spirit, through Adam when she conceives a child. She channels spirit into human form by giving birth. Thus, she begins her spiritual awakening. Through her creative power, Eve brings spirit to earth. Through Adam's soul-activated love and service, her Divine Father connection enlivens. She also becomes an agent of God's divine plan.

> **On the First Mother's Day, Eve's giving birth is humanity's first spiritual embodiment.**

Together, Adam and Eve lead humanity to their divine natures through the profound gifts of family. They learn transcension of self by serving each other. Parenting teaches them the integration of their earthly and divine natures.

CO-CREATION

THE DEMISE OF THE FAMILY

Tragically, we are living at a time that is witnessing the demise of the family. For the first time in recent history, the family is in danger of extinction. According to the recent census, only twenty-five percent of the population live in a nuclear family. Only forty percent of couples decide to marry.

This is the lowest in modern history. Since civilization is based on the family, the family's demise is alarming. Families are where children learn healthy self-construction, morality, conscience, relationships, and male/female models.

Healthy commitment is a sign of adulthood. Is the nation in arrested development? By avoiding long-term commitment, are we seeking instant gratification? Are we so traumatized by parental models that we are afraid of marriage?

Children in single-parent homes are at risk. Seventy-five percent of them experience poverty by age eleven vs. twenty percent of children in two parent families. Children in single-parent homes are more likely to give birth out of wedlock, perpetuating the cycle of alienation. These children are more likely to break the law.

To remedy the loss of the nuclear family, we can teach healthy parenting skills. We can educate children regarding healthy social-roles and deep gender-essences. We can provide good models of how to be male and female. Personally, each of us can wield our love and power with conscious integrity. We can monitor when we slip into polarized thinking and feeling.

We have manifested our technological skills. Now, we must develop our emotional bodies and relationships. Our psychological, social, and spiritual skills are lagging. Our spirit needs renewal.

During this period in history, it is difficult to have an intimate, loving relationship. Gender wars are insidious. They gain internal standing within the individual in toxic self-talk. Separation consciousness creates wars of all kinds, both global and psychological.

Today's spiritual initiates have Soul Contracts to heal the fall from grace, the separation between men and women, the loss of soul embodiment on our planet. The survival of the planet depends upon moving from a gender model of oppression to co-creation.

THE NEW WISDOM AGE

We are on the threshold of a new cycle. The karma between matriarchy and patriarchy is cleansed. There is an opportunity for the New Wisdom Age of shared power. Co-creation between males and females is the new way.

The system of hierarchical power is obsolete. Co-creation skills from the matriarchy before its corruption are needed. Women could facilitate the healing. However, they still have far-memory of the hazards of personal power. To re-engage personal power today is subconsciously terrifying for many women.

WOMAN'S FEAR OF POWER

Many women have difficulty forgiving themselves for being powerful.

In addition, society has persecuted women for thousands of years. A woman has an ingrained, subconscious program in her DNA with far-memory of being hanged, burned, guillotined, banished, and shunned for her powers of healing, prophecy, spiritual vision, and giving birth. The deep programming of collective memory makes it difficult for women to risk being powerful again.

FORGIVING WOMAN'S POWER

At this moment in history, both genders are learning to forgive woman her power. A woman needs to make her power safe for herself and for men. She needs genuine humility and wisdom to manage her great creativity without abuse. Copying male-modeled violence doesn't work.

For a man to allow a woman to be powerful activates man's intrinsic nature to be merciful and loving. His forgiveness of a woman's power unites him with his deep gender-essence. Absorbed in spirit, he is then free of burdensome ego-games.

For a woman to reach into her power is as terrifying as death. For a man to reach into his love, surrender, and mercy is equally terrifying. However, for a woman to deny her power and for a man to deny his love defies their true, deep gender-essences. And, as history demonstrates, imbalance doesn't work. The Yin/Yang Wheel must turn.

Today, there are few models of healthy male/female deep gender-essence. We are still in the aftermath of the gender revolution from the 1960s. The old models are gone. The new models aren't here yet. Women are still male-modeling for success in the marketplace. Men are lost in a fog, lacking clarity of their deep gender-essence.

MEN'S FEAR OF WOMEN'S POWER

Men's fear of women's power is a profound issue. Only men can resolve their disowned fear by self-reflection and self-forgiveness. Redemption comes through honest self-interview about feelings and emotions. A hazard is polarizing from superiority to self-loathing. Getting lost in the weeds of self-destructive behavior serves no one.

Men can learn emotional medicine: naming emotions, processing toxic feelings, and transmuting them. By claiming their deep gender-essence, their sensitive feeling nature, men can "balance their shields." Men can honor their innate talents for love, forgiveness, and mercy—and even their sweetness. It takes courage for a man to be whole in today's world. Ownership of deep male-essence is rare.

In old age, Goethe said, "I finally realized that my whole life I was designed to serve a woman." When the man surrenders to serving the woman, he cracks the code inside his gender-essence and in the woman's heart. She then surrenders to serve him. Selfless service within healthy boundaries is the healing balm for both genders.

National fatherhood initiatives and local groups such as Promise Keepers begin to restore contemporary father's confidence in his ability to love. For successful family life, fathers need parenting, relationship, and anger-management skills.

Increasing numbers of young men emerging in the culture are demonstrating the integration of their deep male-essence. These men will become the cultural models for the new male.

THE HEALTHY MALE

The strong male lifts the weak. The irrational act of loving-service moves the man beyond his surface mode of power games and ego competition. Love requires transcending the earthly linear, left-brain, factual mind. Adam's finding food for his family is deeply motivated by love which integrates him with his divine nature.

> **Man's deep gender-essence is love.**
>
> **This is modeled by Adam's serving his family and by Joseph's mercy for Mary.**

Men can forgive women for the jealousy and fear she creates in him. He can transcend his illusions and drop his ego separation.

Men can heal the illusion that women rob his power. The man judges the woman from his ignorance. His forgiveness is not only for her power—but also for his ignorance of his own deep gender-essence design.

Sin is separation. Separation from truth creates illusion. The man can't blame the woman for her deep gender-essence or her biological construction. A larger Creator than woman is responsible for gender differences.

Honoring and transcending gender connects us with our Creator, restoring unity consciousness and humility.

If you are a man suppressing your feelings and vulnerability, rather than avoidance, practice going into the feelings. Learn sensitivity training. Practice reflective listening, naming your partners emotions with empathy. Learn to transmute volatile emotions rather than act-out or repress.

THE HEALTHY FEMALE

If you are a woman holding back or confused about your power, face the fear. Nurture yourself. Learn self-parenting skills to heal unhealthy internal helpless/hopeless voices. Find a career mentor. Network with other like-minded women. Identify successful examples of healthy female power in the world.

> **Women's deep-essence is creative power.**
>
> **This is modeled by Eve's ability to give birth and in Mary's truth-telling to Joseph.**

For too long, women have male-modeled in their attempt to penetrate the glass ceiling. Instead, they can learn focused mind to replace self-righteous willfulness. Women can embrace their self-affirming creative power. However, that enormous power must be centered in divine Source, rather than earthly ego. Using the God Ladder helps a woman to balance her power in a healthy way. Too often a woman's creative power turns inward to anger or depression.

WHOLENESS MANDATE

Societal images of women as weak doormats and men as aggressive barbarians are disconcerting. It's not easy for a man to surrender into loving vulnerablility or for a woman to own her power. Each gender is challenged by societal ignorance.

Yet, each gender can reclaim its full birthright of love and power. In the battle between matriarchy and patriarchy, no one wins. Negative karma always comes to Light. Jean Shinoda Bolen's book *Urgent Message from the Mother: Gather the Women, Save the World* offers some important insights and tools for both men and women to co-create the future.

Today's plethora of single-parenting is a generational Soul Contract to claim dominion over both love and power, both yin and yang. A single parent takes responsibility for developing both male and female principles.

When two parents work, each parent must be both loving and powerful. Parents must share in child care and domestic duties. For success, parents must co-create as a team.

There is a soul-call for both genders to balance love and power—psychologically, socially, and spiritually.

DIVINE SELVES EMERGING

There is a collective readiness to revamp both genders. Listening to the still small voice of the soul in a wind-tunnel of false images and ego is not easy. But, unhealthy ego leads to abuse of power.

Haven't we had enough grandiosity? Male-principle action derangement has unspooled our finances, our governments, and our nervous systems.

The Wheel always turns. It is time to claim the divine selfhood within both genders. The divine equipment on your God Ladder includes: intuition, soul, spirit, and Universal God Source. In the divine realm, the earthly male-principle translates into your spiritual self. The earthly female-principle vibrates in the divine realm as your soul.

The divine worlds teach wisdom skills of unity, co-operation, collaboration, and compromise. Values evolve from "me" to "we." Rather than self-centeredness, the collective good is honored. Beyond selfish motive, care is given to serving the evolution of the human family. Service is considered a privilege.

Wisdom asks: How do we work together to solve problems? Serving the generational Soul Contract for the evolution of humanity is wildly more exciting than the linear function of me-me-me. With the wisdom of our divine selves, men and women can co-create the future together. This is a job for the Wise Man and the Wise Woman.

EVOLUTIONARY CHOICE-POINT

Humanity is at an evolutionary choice-point. The world has taken the male-action principle to unhealthy extremes of misapplication and over-stimulation.

In the excess yang energy, time and space have contracted. We live in a global village with instant communication connecting people across the world. Global intensity has exponentially increased, along with the complexity of global and personal problems.

As a grandmother, I am deeply concerned for the future. We desperately need our men and women working together in families as healthy models for our children. It's time for families to value and to foster wisdom skills of collaboration and co-operation.

We need the Wise Man and Wise Woman to lead the way on the Lighted Path of human evolution. Going into the future, we need both the male light saber opening the way and the female basket collecting the valuables.

The obstacle to men's evolution is their mind and willfulness. The obstacle to women's evolution is their emotions and complexity.

Both genders need transcension skills for healthy selfhood, for parenting, and for co-creation. Both men and women need conscious ownership of their soul and spiritual selfhood. It's time to claim our divine birthright. The Wise Man and the Wise Woman are needed to lead our children forward.

THE WISE MAN AND THE WISE WOMAN

DIVINE FATHER, DIVINE MOTHER

In the divine realm, the female face of God is your soul, Divine Mother. Her voice is full of love, nurturing, compassion, and forgiveness. She guides you through the personal ups and downs of daily living. Her essence is love.

She teaches you how to apply and to integrate the 7 domains of your God Ladder: **physical, emotional, mental, intuitional, soul, spiritual, and Universal God Source.** These are the 7 aspects of what it is to be human. She helps you to decode life's complexity.

The male face of God is your spiritual self, Divine Father. He reveals the laws and limits that define both earthly and divine life. He delivers strength and divine law. He brings the spiritual warrior and right-action framed by divine truth. He teaches respect, detachment, and transcension of personal self. His essence is truth.

Divine Mother shows you how to assemble earthly selfhood with healthy physical, emotional, and mental skills. She helps you to create healthy ego. She deals with the limits of earthly duality.

Divine Father teaches you how to transcend earthly selfhood and duality, so you don't become attached to your "achievements." Instead, you expand your personal identity to include impersonal, eternal realities. **Through non-attachment skills, he ensures that you don't confuse your life with your identity**. He deals with divine, universal realities.

By consciously accessing Divine Mother and Divine Father, you learn to pick-up your ego identities and to put them down. Attachments don't run you. You learn service to the highest good of each moment.

Everyone needs clear access to both their soul (female) and spirit (male) to avoid grandiosity, self-loathing, ignorance, or cynicism. Consciously using your divine equipment keeps you humble and hopeful. It helps you to operate within healthy boundaries so your ego doesn't get out of control.

With Divine Mother, your soul's healthy conscience guides you to avoid action abuse—whether its calendar, cyber, or clock. You surrender to healthy limits. You respect the laws, both earthly and divine. To operate without conscience is to be without soul.

With Divine Father, your spiritual self helps you to see the larger picture beyond your selfish interest. Higher on the God Ladder, your view expands to see beyond limited earthly time and space. You tap into universal archetypes and divine law.

Divine Father guides you to trust God's Plan beyond your own. Through him, you gain conscious entry to your 7th rung Universal God Source with its unlimited infinite energy, intelligence, resource, renewal, and supply.

A complete God Ladder—consciously using both your divine and your earthly equipment—keeps you balanced throughout life. When you honor divine principles of love and truth, you achieve spiritual adulthood. The adult respects the limit of each rung on the God Ladder with wise use of power. There can be no Peter Pans or co-dependents.

YOUR EARTHLY AND DIVINE NATURES

Your earthly equipment comprises the lower 3 rungs of your God Ladder. Each rung is a discrete reality domain with its own limits and powers.

- Your earthly realm includes your: **physical, emotional, and mental bodies.**
- These worlds are limited by time and space.
- They exist below the Psychic Barrier. The Psychic Barrier separates the unlimited divine realm from the limited earthly reality on your God Ladder.
- The three domains of your earthly realm are highly dualized. Duality ensures plenty of action, conflict, and imperfection in the endless dialogue between yin and yang.
- Earthly duality also ensures resistance and friction between the opposites: yours/mine; hot/cold; peace/war; summer/winter; male/female; up/down; good/bad.
- The laws of your earthly equipment include: duality, limitation, imperfection, conditionality, impermanence, change, transience, and the personal.
- By contrast to the divine realm, the earthly realm is extremely contracted, yang energy.
- At the 1st rung, the divine yin energy from the 7th rung is so compacted into yang energy that it is tangible and visible in the world of matter.

Your divine equipment comprises the upper 4 rungs of your God Ladder.

- The divine realm includes your: **intuition, soul, spirit, and Universal God Source.**
- These worlds are not limited by time or space.
- They exist above the Psychic Barrier.
- These 4 domains on your God Ladder are non-dual, non-polarized, non-oppositional, non-local, unlimited.
- The laws of your divine equipment include: non-duality, unity, oneness, infinity, eternity, unchanging, unconditional, impersonal, universal, perfection, omnipresence, omniscience, and omnipotence.
- The divine realm is expanded, extreme yin energy.

- These worlds are so expanded in yin energy that they are invisible and intangible. Earthly form is deconstructed and released into spirit. Energy essence is all that remains of form at your 7th rung.

THE GOD LADDER, SPIRITUAL TECHNOLOGY

The God Ladder is a spiritual technology mapping what it is to be human. With clarity, you can access the entirety of your being, your wholeness. Yes, even your holiness.

The God Ladder gives practical skills to integrate your earthly and divine natures. It keeps you grounded to deal with today's accelerated world as a balanced, spiritual adult. Guarding against spiritual escapism, the God Ladder insures your integrity.

Using the God Ladder helps both men and women to balance their power in a healthy way. Honest self-interview at each rung of the ladder brings clarity regarding any false beliefs or illusions.

The voice of God is different at each rung of the ladder. Your soul is the voice of kindness that never leaves. She is very personal and always loving. The voice of your 6th rung spirit is impersonal truth. At times, it can feel ruthless in its radiance. It does not kiss the oweee to make it better.

The God Ladder teaches discernment to understand the many realities of being human. You learn to decipher earthly reality in the light of eternity. You gain participatory divinity in a grounded, integrated way that keeps you humble.

The beauty of the God Ladder is that it keeps you honest. The laws, powers, hazards, and limits of each of the 7 domains of human life vary. With clarity, you awaken to where your identity is focalized on the God Ladder at any given moment in the day. If you are false-godding from the dualized world of limited time and space, you can self-correct.

Your true and ultimate identity is on the 7th Rung of God Source. The Great Immensity created you and all that is. Discover True Source and you never again are helpless and hopeless.

THE GOD LADDER GRAPHIC

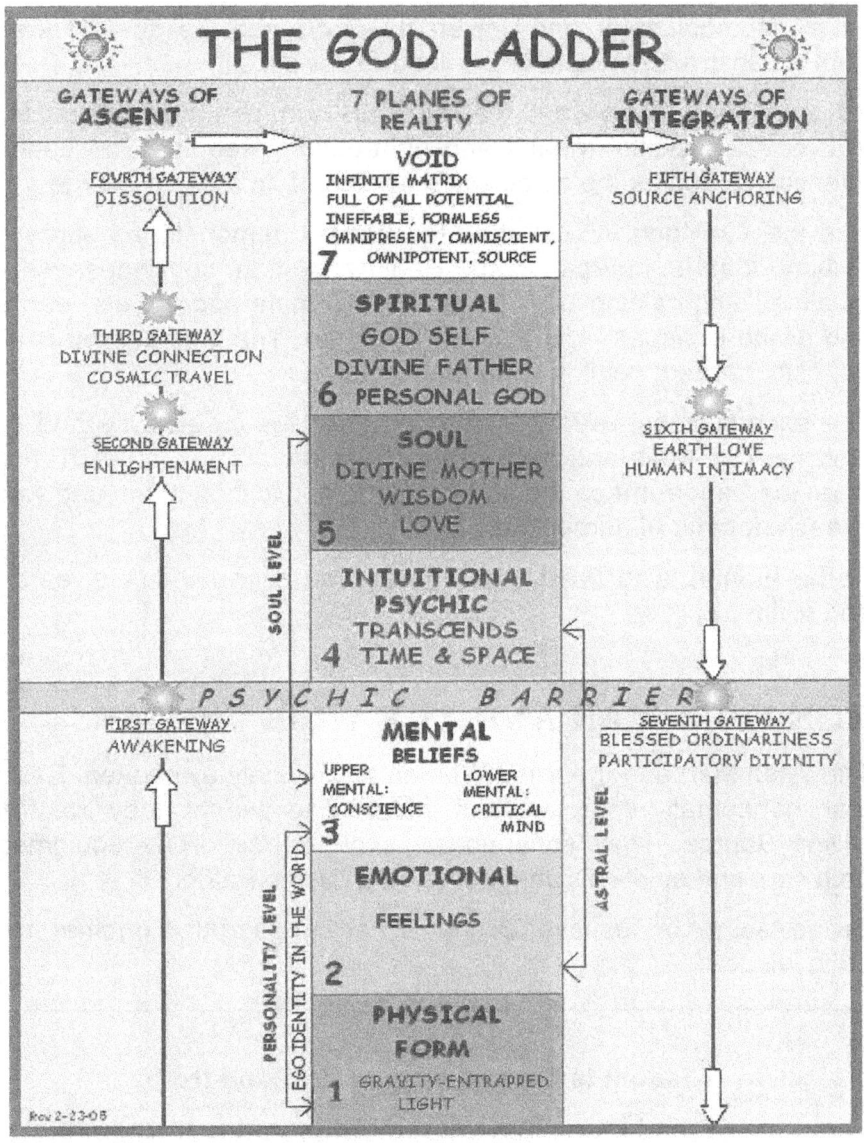

SPIRITUAL INTEGRATION

With spiritual adulthood, you learn the limits, hazards, gifts, and powers of each of your 7 domains: physical, emotional, mental, intuitional, soul, spirit, and Universal God Source. Spirituality moves from an abstract principle into a lived experience.

As you explore each world, you study its right use and applications. You develop skillful means and right-action. Regular God Ladder attention remedies the complaint that there's no adult in charge.

Like the Yin-Yang Wheel, the God Ladder demonstrates supreme polarity that is non-polarized. Healthy human consciousness is balanced—containing both yin and yang, male and female, earthly and divine energies—dynamically engaged. The God Ladder is not oppositionalized, yet it is supremely polar.

The exchange between male/female energies creates life and the God Ladder. Male and female principles reconfigure at each rung. The God Ladder maps the state-specific application of yin and yang in each domain of human life.

To be human is to live at the intersection of male/female, earthly and divine realities.

THE WISE MAN AND THE WISE WOMAN

The Wise Man and the Wise Woman are divinely awakened. Rather than horizontally sourcing from people and events, they live from Divine Source. They continuously access their divine equipment, both soul and spirit—Divine Mother and Divine Father.

Divine Mother brings love; Divine Father brings truth. Together, they bring wisdom.

Wisdom is the marriage of love and truth.

When I know that I am nothing, that is truth.
When I know that I am everything, that is love.

When I flow between the two, that is wisdom.

Wisdom Keepers move energies horizontally in the earthly worlds and vertically in the divine worlds. Energies circulate through them on the God Ladder. Male and female energies actively engage inside and outside of them. They integrate Divine Mother and Divine Father into daily life. Earthly and divine realms co-create in the dialogue of being human.

Wisdom involves the circulation of energies. A frozen state of stasis blocks the natural flow of God Ladder dynamics. Health is energy exchange—between love and truth; male and female; earthly and divine; inhale and exhale.

Wisdom Keepers have conscious skills in the right use of their earthly physical, emotional, and mental powers. They also understand their divine powers: intuition, soul, spirit, and Universal God Source.

Learning the laws and limits of the 7 domains teaches wisdom. Exercising the gifts and powers of the rungs wisely is right action.

Use your God Ladder to understand where your consciousness is focused at any given moment. Once you are aware, you have power to change, your thoughts, words, and deeds. You have power to change your life and your future.

The God Ladder provides maps, models, methods, and mentoring for wisdom training. It is consciousness aerobics to exercise all your equipment—both earthly and divine. The God Ladder reunites you with your divinity, your holiness.

The Wise Man and Wise Woman are essential to civilization. Wisdom is needed for humanity to move forward into the New Wisdom Age.

THE COMPLETE HUMAN

Each of the 7 rungs is a unique world with its own training program. When your identity focalizes on a particular rung, you must digest, assimilate, and integrate its agenda. Then, you transcend that domain and move to the next. At each level of the God Ladder, your identity expands, until it merges with the Universal God Source of the 7th rung.

The beauty of being human is that you can access both earthly and divine realms. However, your complete anatomy must be understood and managed properly. The conditional earthly and unconditional divine realms are opposites that require very different skills on the God Ladder.

Your earthly and divine equipment have radically different Rule Books and Operating Manuals. They have different powers, laws, limits, and hazards. They have different boundaries and entitlements.

How do you grow large enough to embrace the opposites—earthly duality and divine non-duality? How do you honor the limits of earthly transience and the unlimited, infinite, eternal divine, simultaneously?! How do you own the male and female inside you? How do you co-create with warring factions of yours and mine in the world?

These are not easy questions. Working with your complete anatomy on the God Ladder provides some answers. Earthly duality and divine non-duality are your teachers. Divine Mother and Divine Father are your guides. Expanding your identity to contain the opposites with conscious skill is the goal.

This is the journey of enlightened consciousness.

GOD LADDER INTEGRATION

When you can consciously dialogue among your many parts, you have healthy self-integration. Life's developmental curriculum repeatedly reiterates the skills for healthy self-construction, at each rung of the God Ladder: physical, emotional, mental, intuition, soul, spirit, and Universal God Source.

Healthy self-construction includes knowledge of:

> Healthy boundaries and limits; entitlement; self-interview; objective naming skills; truth-telling; communication; active-listening with empathy; healthy confrontation; impulse control; enlistment skills; and conflict resolution skills.

God Ladder exercises teach healthy self-parenting using these basic skills at every rung.

In each domain, you explore these skills and their healthy application. You dialogue with the voices in each domain. Along with Divine Mother, your soul, you carefully listen to their complaints and issues—taking time to examine conflicts until you find resolution.

The rungs also dialogue with each other while you self-witness. Sometimes, there is a cacophony of voices. Your body wants one thing, your emotions another, and your mind a third!

You learn to self-parent—your body, your emotions, your mental beliefs, your intuitions, your soul, and your spirit. Your Divine Parents referee and mediate conflicting internal voices. Rather than abstract concepts, Divine Mother and Divine Father become integral parts of your daily dialogues. Sometimes, the soul's love is the answer. Other times, spirit's detachment and transcension are the answer.

Valuing the wisdom of your Divine Parents, you run your decisions past them. You ask, "What would my soul say in this situation? How would Divine Father see it?"

You enlist their insight regarding your choices. You discuss your thoughts, feelings, appetites, energies, and life events. Nothing is too small to discuss with them. If something bothers you and it flags your attention, it's time to go "upstairs" for divine perspective. You install a hot-line for daily talks, perspective, advice, and renewal.

At each rung, illusions and attachments gradually dissolve as you transcend on the journey to God union. You walk the Wisdom Way with your Divine Parents. You are no longer alone.

DIVINE SELF-PARENTING

With so many dysfunctional families, we have lost healthy parenting models in society. You can use Divine Mother and Divine Father to remedy the deficit. Regardless of your childhood models, you can learn healthy parenting through divine self-parenting.

Actively engage your soul and your spirit—Divine Mother and Divine Father. Access them internally in meditation and throughout the day. They will guide you. Use Sarah Young's wonderful book *Jesus Calling* for daily divine sustenance. Unity's *Daily Word* is also divinely inspired.

The God Ladder is a fabulous tool for divine self-parenting. It teaches healthy self-construction and self-transcension. God Ladder workouts expand your identity to include both your earthly and divine natures.

Transcending your earthly ego is the journey of divine self-parenting. The irony is, first you must develop a healthy ego before you can transcend it!

Divine Mother and Divine Father guide you in digesting, assimilating, and integrating earthly life; ultimately, so you can transcend it. You learn to pick-up your physical appetites, emotions, and beliefs—and to put them down. Just as a two-year old learns to contract and expand muscles by dropping objects and by potty training, you learn to open and close earthly attachments. You learn when to pick-up your ego and when to put it down.

The God Ladder helps you to name your experience objectively—whether in this life or a past life. When you place your experience in its proper domain among the 7 rungs, you gain perspective. You understand healthy limits and powers; causes and dynamics. With conscious, clear discernment, you gain wisdom.

For example, if you are upset emotionally, you can track it back to your physical biochemistry—something you ate, perhaps; or, to a false belief in your subconscious mind—that "life is hopeless and you are hopeless," perhaps; or, to an earlier unresolved emotional trauma, perhaps. Or, with advanced skills, you can transcend earthly space/time, tracking the root cause of a problem to past lives and relationships, perhaps.

> **Right-action varies with each event and domain:
> physical, emotional, mental, intuition, soul, spirit,
> Universal God Source.**

Awakening your Divine Feminine (soul) and Divine Masculine (spirit) brings healthy concern for both the whole and the parts. You begin to see how all the rungs of the God Ladder work together. In daily life, you begin to include both "me" and "we." You value the community good, along with your personal good.

You learn right motive as you begin to ask, "What is for the highest good of all involved, including me?" With pure motive, you can serve the divine plan more clearly. As your identity expands to contain both earthly and divine realms, you become an agent of God, a Wise One.

SELF-WITNESSING

Becoming conscious in the 7 rungs of your God Ladder, you receive tangible, real-life insight into worlds that previously were only abstract concepts. You gain cellular knowledge of the subtle, energy differences among the domains.

Awareness of duality helps you to transcend it, even while you are immersed in it. The simple act of self-witnessing on all seven rungs of your God Ladder—physical, emotional, mental, intuitional, soul, spiritual, and Universal Source—brings enlightenment to the planet.

Objective, detached naming without toxic blaming is clear witnessing. Simply, name your experience throughout the day. Notice where your identity is focalized on the God Ladder. Where are you stuck?

Begin to ask "Who am I?" each moment throughout the day. Observe where you are attached. Where is the energy most intense on your God Ladder? Ask,

- Am I identified with my physical appetites?
- Am I attached to my emotions? Are they running my life?
- Am I rigid in my beliefs? Am I brain-washed by my family, religion, or the collective?
- Do I feel invaded by psychic energies from others? Am I so sensitive that I take-on other people's energies?
- Am I fixated in the dream I had last night? Dreams are often messages from your soul.
- What does my conscience say is right-action?

- Is my spirit troubled? What does my spirit need to find peace? Am I detached and clear? Or am I ensnared in duality, still digesting yesterday's episode?

Over time, you anchor witnesses on each rung of your God Ladder. Witnesses stand like hall monitors in each domain helping you to gather information. They guide the heavy traffic of your awakening as you learn the rules of each world.

Lingering after all the "Who am I?" questions, there remains the non-attached witness presiding over all the hall monitors. You begin to ask, "Who stands behind the curtain running this show!? Who witnesses the witnesses?!"

The one witness who simultaneously knows all seven levels of your God Ladder life-experience is your personal spark of God. This Divine Witness stands untouched, like the sky behind the moving clouds of your life. This is your 7th rung Universal God Source.

By clearly witnessing your seven rungs throughout the day, you consciously bring God to earth. God Ladder self-witnessing strengthens your connection to your Divine Witness.

Everyone has a God spark in them. However, not everyone is conscious of their Divine Source. The God Ladder provides enlightened understanding of all your parts and how they work together.

SPIRITUAL AWAKENING

Your spiritual awakening brings divine energy to the entire planet as the vibration lifts in your body and your life. God consciousness emerges from Source down the God Ladder into manifest, earthly form—anchoring for the collective in your unique perspective, design, energy imprint, and cellular knowledge.

You can either be conscious or unconscious of the descent of spirit into matter. When you identify with matter at the expense of spirit, unconsciousness allows the sin of separation from your Divine Source.

BEYOND POLARIZING

Conscious awakening frees you to become simultaneously aware of both matter and spirit, yours and mine, good and bad, male and female—without polarizing or otherating. With practice, you can clearly discern without judgmentalness. You can name the pain without toxic shaming.

If you don't oppositionalize, you can stand in the integrity of your personal view, while keeping your energy clear to understand the other's view. There is no enemy in the room. With a soft heart, you speak from an "us" space. You move from willfulness to willingness, from humiliation to humility.

When your identity expands to include the other person, you literally know the other as yourself. Your consciousness embraces both spirit and matter; divine and human; male and female; self and other. Transcending separation, you don't get lost in the doo-doo duality.

When you ascend your God Ladder, you see through your God Glasses of co-creation. From higher on your God Ladder, your perspective widens to reveal new solutions. Experiencing infinite resource and supply from your 7th rung Universal God Source breaks the hypnotic trance of earthly helpless/hopeless thinking. Sometimes, your earthly vision needs divine renewal.

For dominion, you must operate and serve both your earthly and divine natures. Gender differences, marriage, and family help you to do that. They help you to identify polarized consciousness, to remedy it, and to transcend duality. Relationships are where you spiritually awaken.

THE OPPOSITES

The two realms—earthly and divine—are opposites, yet interwoven in the human journey. Wholeness mandates honoring both your limited and unlimited natures. To walk in the Wisdom Way, you must learn how to operate and to integrate this complex equipment.

The God Ladder teaches the horizontal integration of your earthly self with the "other" in linear time and space. You also learn the vertical integration of your earthly duality with your non-dualized, perfect, timeless, divine energies.

Both horizontal and vertical integration are needed for balanced living as a spiritual adult. Without this God Ladder awareness, many people false-god from horizontal events and people.

Indeed, to be human is to live at the intersection of spirit and matter. Some would say we are crucified on the cross of spirit and matter. As the poet T. S. Elliot says, we are "pinned and wriggling on the wall" of what it is to be human in God's "butterfly" collection!

BOTH/AND EMBRACE

With spiritual adulthood, rather than either/or polarizing, mature consciousness expands to embrace the both/and. You see the other as an aspect of yourself. You actually know yourself as God as well as the butterfly—simultaneously.

With participatory divinity, you are the creator and the creation—both immanent and transcendent, the sacred and the profane. God Ladder consciousness embraces both your earthly imperfection and your divine perfection in the lived-experience of being human.

There is integration and balance. Rather than oppositionalizing heaven and earth in victim/tyrant, good/bad dualized scripts, you grow large enough to contain both the yin and the yang, male and female, earthly and divine.

When you affirm both your earthly and your divine natures, you move from limited either/or consciousness to more inclusive both/and consciousness. **Like the Yin-Yang Wheel, the God Ladder honors both the duality and the unity.**

Your entire God Ladder—all 7 rungs—includes both your earthly and divine natures. **This is your Supreme Ultimate identity while you are on earth**.

To be a complete human, you need access to both your male and female principles as they reformat in both your earthly and divine natures. Right-action changes according to events. One occasion may require your inner female to listen. Another occasion may require your outer male to act.

The male and female energies continuously interact in the dialogue between your earthly and divine bodies. Their fecundity creates life. Divine Mother and Divine Father guide you in the Wisdom Way. Love and truth light the path.

For health and fitness, the Wise One exercises a complete God Ladder.

GENDER HALL OF MIRRORS

The gender dance creates male/female energies dialoguing in reversals as you ascend the God Ladder. Earthly gender-essence flips with social roles.

At the internal earthly level, the deep female-essence is power; the male gender-essence is love. If you move to the social playing-field, the external role of woman is love; the male is power.

At the divine level, the female soul and male spirit engage again. The receptive female soul's love is integrative; while the active male spirit transcends into egoless, universal detachment.

Like Russian dolls, images of male and female nest inside each other. Yin and yang merge and emerge into new forms. As you ascend the God Ladder, is the man closer to God—or is woman?

Gender essences rebound in a complex Hall of Mirrors. If God is male, at some point you ask "Who is God's mother?" Ha! God must be laughing at human mind-stuff confusion. The gender dance can degenerate to gender dueling.

GOD LADDER KOAN

Question: Who's on top? Who's on the bottom? Yin or Yang? Male or female?

God Ladder answer: They both are! There's that co-creation again!

God Ladder work opens linear space/time duality into simultaneity. God is androgynous plus—extending beyond gender duality. The ultimate Divine Source is non-dual.

Both genders coexist inside each of us. There is no competition, no winning, no top, no bottom—only co-creation.

Fruitless sophistry leads to arrested development in mind games at the third rung of the God Ladder—the mental body. "Who knows? Who cares? Who witnesses?" is a deeper question exploring self-inquiry and identity.

"Who am I?" is the ultimate question. Your identity reconfigures and expands at every rung of the God Ladder: physical, emotional, mental, intuition, soul, spirit, and Universal God Source.

DIVINE TRANSCENSION

When you expand your identity to include the Nothingness, you move into the 7th rung of no-thingness. Beyond the realm of mind, you enter divine union. The price of entry is surrendering your mind. Even attachment to your personal God-concepts must go in the Great Dissolve of the 7th rung.

Disengaging from polarity is liberating. Your identity expands beyond personal attachments to merge with Universal God Source. You unite with the Divine Matrix, Primal Energy, the Fertile Void—a veritable warehouse of deconstructed, pure essences.

This is your powerhouse of infinite supply, intelligence, support, refuge, and renewal. This is the same Source that creates All That Is—universes, worlds, rivers, mountains, oceans, plants, animals, and humans.

With divine transcension, you shift from horizontally sourcing through earthly events and people. As your consciousness expands, you true-source from your Universal Source. You no longer false-god from people or events. A whole new dimension opens. You become personally contained and universally sustained.

However, transcendent states have their hazards. You certainly can't pay your bills or drive your car in nirvikalpa samadhi. And, there's always the pesky business of earning a living. As Jack Kornfield says, *After the Ecstasy, the Laundry*!

Different from spiritual escapism, God Ladder transcension is enlightened understanding of the values and limits of both duality and non-duality. Transcension is not spiritual by-pass, escaping into fantasy land, or skipping the hard work of facing limits.

The spiritual adult respects the laws and the limits. Transcension is not the same as numbing-out or avoidant behavior. The 7th rung is not glamorized at the expense of earthly life.

Rather, God Ladder transcension honors right-action within each domain. Transcension deals with adult responsibilities and maintains integrity. Centering, balancing, grounding, integration, and service are important keys in God Ladder aerobics.

THE WISDOM WAY

How do you grow large enough to embrace the opposites in transcension? Regular God Ladder work builds the necessary spiritual muscles. Over time, your identity expands to contain the paradox of earthly duality and divine union, simultaneously.

You become conscious of the either/or and the both/and living inside you. Your identity expands to embrace them, simultaneously. You become comfortable with both the male and female principles; yin and yang energies; earthly and divine; the everything and the nothing.

With spiritual adulthood, you cross the duality divide. You look through earthly and divine eyes, simultaneously. You shift from seeing only "either/or." Instead, you see through "both/and" eyes.

As your treasured concepts and ideas dissolve in the Divine Light, you grow beyond "being right." You surrender your ego and your mind to the Great Unknowing in the move from earthly duality to transcension.

Relationship, parenting, and family teach the Wisdom Way. In relationship, monitor when your energies polarize into self/other opposition. Internal scripts such as, "I have the one right way and the other is wrong" can indicate that you have fallen into the doo-doo duality trap.

If you are demonizing your opponent, you may not be balanced on your God Ladder. Self-witnessing all 7 rungs helps you to awaken from the earthly trance.

Transcension is when you realize that the other person is part of you. Your identity expands to include "the other." The unity of this wholeness clears the polarized energy through heart-centered communication.

The conjoining of heaven and earth is the Wisdom Way.

CONSCIOUS PARENTING

Through conscious God Ladder work, you become a Wisdom Keeper. By understanding healthy selfhood and divine self-parenting, you can parent your own children more effectively.

I have written a number of books to help you with practical skills to consciously own and operate your entire God Ladder. See *For Further Study* at the end of this book for a complete list of my books. Also, see www.GatewayUniversity.org.

For specific earthly and divine God Ladder skills, I especially recommend:

- *Self-Interview: Using Your God Ladder for Self-Discovery*
- *Reinventing God: God Discovery, Personally and Historically*
- *Divine Father—Your God: Deepening Your God Connection*
- *Divine Mother—Your Soul: Deepening Your Soul Connection*

Parenting has a built-in God Ladder. It teaches you healthy self-construction, selfless service, self transcension, and co-creation. Parenting helps you to evolve up your God Ladder. Families are the most spiritual work on the planet!

As we enter the New Wisdom Age, our families deliver important developmental curriculum—both earthly and divine. We need healthy families to bring the next generation of Wise Men and Wise Women.

THE PARENT'S JOURNEY

THE KING AND QUEEN

Fatherhood and motherhood are the direct experience of the king and queen archetypes. Parenting creates a kingdom. Children are the king and queen's "subjects."

However, benevolent rulership is often difficult to achieve on the earthly plane of duality that guarantees flaws. Life offers complex self-development and spiritual lessons with age and growth.

DEVELOPMENT AND IDENTITY EXPANSION

The child's developmental task is self-construction and creating personal ego. The job of childhood is to be self-centered and self-interested. In childhood, we create ego to transcend it later in life!

As we have seen, healthy parenting involves teaching the child healthy self-construction including the following skills:

> Boundaries and limits; entitlement; self-interview; objective naming; truth-telling; communication; active-listening with empathy; confrontation; impulse control; enlistment; and conflict resolution.

The child needs healthy selfhood to develop autonomy.

Through teenage rebellion, the child individuates from mom/dad and defines herself independently. With the hormonal agenda and pair-bonding, the self-discovery process complexifies. Relationship skills move onto center-stage.

Marriage expands personal identity when you learn to care for someone beyond yourself. Committing to another requires that you go deeper in love skills, transcending self-interest to include your partner.

Parenting stretches your identity even further. In parenting, you transcend personal ego by caring for your child. The opportunities for selfless giving are endless. Children are demanding. They don't wait. The baby is shamelessly self-centered, piggish for the mother's breast, gobbling everyone's attention.

An ego battle ensues inside both parents. The mother sacrifices her body, time, and energy to the baby. The father sacrifices time, energy, and his wife to his baby's demands for attention. Love wins out in family life—or you lose your sanity!

At each level of development, life has built-in curriculum to teach right use of power and expanded identity. Eventually, in senior status, your identity expands to include life beyond death. Death is the ultimate identity crisis!

With each identity expansion, you embrace more of your divine self.

SELF-TRANSCENSION

You can't be married long without experiencing the sin of separation. Soon, you see your partner as shockingly different from yourself. Someone once joked, "You get married so you have someone to blame. It's more convenient than blaming yourself!"

However, marriage also has the potential to heal separation consciousness. Marriage is a call to transcend the self. You serve a larger value of lifetime love.

Rather than seeing your partner as the enemy, you build a communication bridge connecting the two of you. With healthy communication, you love both yourself and your partner. On the altar of relationship, your life is consecrated. You honor the gift of loving beyond yourself.

Across time, there's a softening of hard edges. Perhaps, you have seen this softening in the faces of long-married couples. They carry a surrendered aliveness and microscopic gratitude. Love has found a way to help them transcend duality.

To move forward in marriage, you must forgive both yourself and your partner. Marriage mandates on-going forgiveness, love, and mercy. Marriage also mandates truth-telling and right use of power. These are jobs for the Wise Man and the Wise Woman. Wisdom helps you to transcend separation through heart-centered, truthful action.

SELFLESS SERVICE

Selfless service is the basic curriculum of parenting. The egoless service of parenting protects against grandiosity. Selfless service is an important shield in balancing your power with love.

Parenting is a sacrificial act, dissolving personal ego. I often hear parents say, "Loving my child is the deepest love I've ever known." The parent's identity expands beyond selfish interest to embrace the family's best interest.

The father's sacrifice is enormous. He gives everything to his family. His love is so great that he would die to protect them in an emergency. Father's strength fortifies family life. He teaches truth-telling and respect for the law. He models Divine Father

The mother's sacrifice is also enormous. Through her nurturing, the child grows. Mother teaches love and conscience. She models the Divine Mother.

Parents act as divine agents of God. Family life provides parents the opportunity to redeem humanity through healthy self-construction, selfless service, and ego transcension.

Parenting is the earthly laboratory where you work-out the limits of your earthly ego: physical, emotional, and mental. Parenting demands the co-creation of love and truth in the right use of power. Families require transcending your ego, using both earthly and divine skills on the journey to wisdom.

It is essential for our children to see healthy fathering and mothering, the Wise Man and the Wise Woman. Marriage and family are the building blocks of civilization. Healthy parenting can redeem humanity.

HONORING FATHER

On Father's Day, we honor the father's loving sacrifice, his burdens, dedication, and contribution to family life. We honor father's social role, his deep gender-essence, and his divinity as a man.

Imagine a world without fathers. Where would we be without father's social-role? His strength, leadership, and protection? Where would the world be without his defense of justice? Where would we be without the man's deep gender-essence? His mercy, love, and forgiveness? Where would we be without his divine ability to transcend selfish interest?

Hold the father principle in your mind's eye. Find the healthy father within you.

What would the world be without these qualities? What would you be without these qualities?

YOUR SOUL CONTRACT

If you are a survivor of child abuse, on Father's Day, it is helpful to understand how Soul Contracts work. Between incarnations, you—in partnership with your divine self and guides—design your Soul Contract for your next life. You make an assessment of your past lives regarding incomplete curriculum. If lessons from past lives were unlearned, you design your next life to complete them.

On Father's Day, we honor the father's loving sacrifice, his burdens, dedication, and contribution to family life. We honor father's social role, his deep gender-essence, and his divinity as a man.

Imagine a world without fathers. Where would we be without father's social-role? His strength, leadership, and protection? Where would the world be without his defense of justice? Where would we be without the man's deep gender-essence? His mercy, love, and forgiveness? Where would we be without his divine ability to transcend selfish interest?

Hold the father principle in your mind's eye. Find the healthy father within you.

What would the world be without these qualities? What would you be without these qualities?

YOUR SOUL CONTRACT

If you are a survivor of child abuse, on Father's Day, it is helpful to understand how Soul Contracts work. Between incarnations, you—in partnership with your divine self and guides—design your Soul Contract for your next life. You make an assessment of your past-lives regarding incomplete curriculum. If lessons from past-lives were unlearned, you design your next life to complete them.

You choose the precise moment of your birth, death, and your parents. There are no accidents. This is precision engineering.

For this lifetime, you choose the perfect, right father to teach your lessons. You choose your father's personality, his station in life, his temperameht, and his basic design—even the locality and culture where you grew up. Your choice is carefully designed to deliver your life-lessons.

Each childhood wound contains wisdom and power—waiting for you to retrieve them. Often, we learn through opposites.

When seen through the eyes of the soul, there are no victims—since you are a creator in your karma and your life-plan. However, when seen through earthly eyes, there are victims—legally, morally, and psychologically.

When you ascend the God Ladder, you look at your earthly life through the eyes of the soul. Both the earthly and divine views are correct. Your job in life is to grow large enough to embrace the opposites—to integrate your earthly and divine natures in co-creation. Your soul assists you in clearing earthly conflicts and illusions.

Understanding the abuser's Soul Contract along with your own can help you to transcend childhood pain and injustice. You may not be conscious of your parental choice before birth. However, you can consciously change your pattern of responding to life as an adult.

TOXIC DAD'S SACRIFICE

When we look at toxic dad's life through the eyes of the soul, we often see a tragically damaged, polarized, emotionally crippled baby-man. If we step into dad's shoes as a child, we can find the damage that was perpetrated upon him by his toxic parents and society. We can feel his pain. We can even see his sad, defensive adaptation to that pain in his toxic selfhood.

What a lot of pain! What agony he suffered! What twisted, poisonous iterations of society and parenting!

Native American Indian wisdom says "Walk a mile in a man's moccasins before you judge him." Once you step into dad's "hurt-locker," it becomes easier to un-bind from him. Through the heart of compassion, you discover space that unlocks your trauma-bind. You see through the eyes of God.

You see your dad as a helpless child of ignorance, doing the best he could with what life gave him. He mustered as much dignity and strength as he could—given his toxic childhood.

You see his sacrifice in coming to earth to experience such pain. As broken as he was, as bereft of healthy skills as he was, he mustered his courage to serve as your father. He gave you a presence to push-off from in your self-discovery journey. Because he stood and provided the pain of resistance, he anchored a psychological landmark allowing you to awaken.

He embodied a model which you can later accept or reject depending upon your Soul Contract. From his reference point, you can get your bearings. You can decode the rest of your psychological scenery.

When you unify with divine love, you find True Love—the only love that will never leave you through growth or death. With Divine Parents—Divine Mother and Divine Father—you find the love that endures the many changes and betrayals of earthly life.

Then, you no longer need to polarize from earthly dad, making him wrong. You have your own internal healthy father archetype. Through Divine Sourcing you can self-parent, redeeming yourself and your own children.

Once you feel your dad's suffering, you can find the healing balm of forgiveness—the place of mercy, compassion, unity, and love. You can transcend the past.

However, because you forgive someone does not mean that you necessarily agree with them. Because you love someone does not mean that you like them. For healthy boundaries, you may choose to maintain a safe distance from a toxic person.

The gift of the healing journey is healthy boundaries. You continuously ask: What is mine? What is yours? What is ours?

You take responsibility for what belongs to you—and no more. You no longer must carry broken people on your back out of guilt. You are free to stand in the light of day, owning your healthy separation and entitlement. You are free to do your part—nothing more, nothing less.

You no longer play God, judging and saving others. Rather, you humbly embrace the limits of what it is to be human. To come here to earth, so heavily immersed in pain and duality is a truly courageous act. It is heroic to be human.

LEARNING THROUGH OPPOSITES

You learn who you are by discovering who you are not. You learn by opposites, comparisons, and contrast.

Because toxic parenting taught you what is not healthy, you now have healthy ownership of yourself—nothing more, nothing less.

You are humbly grateful for the opportunity to witness the love and beauty here. You embrace blessed ordinariness.

Earthly incarnation is sacramental. Through the sacrifice and pain of your toxic parents—and through your own hero's journey—you are freed.

GRATITUDE FOR DAD

Give thanks for your earthly father. Feel gratitude for his sacrifice and selfless service. Present or absent, he gave you the gift of life.

The privilege of human life is one of the greatest gifts in the multiverse. Millions of souls stand waiting for incarnation here. The ticket to ride earth's human journey is rare and valuable beyond measure.

Even the gods are jealous of the human child. The gods exist in abstracted divine realms. They can't access earthly equipment in the way that humans can. The human span of both the earthly and divine realms in the complete God Ladder even surpasses the range of the gods. Without human bodies, the gods do not have the full complement of human powers. To be human is truly a sacred gift.

Give thanks for your life and for the father principle within you. You carry the ability to forgive, to have mercy, and to love beyond reason—beyond separation. You carry Divine Father's gift of transcension.

The wholeness of the holy family lies within each of us. Divine Mother and Divine Father dispense the larger plan. Becoming Wisdom Keepers is our destiny. The Wise Man and the Wise Woman are the evolutionary goal of the Human Experiment.

FORGIVING ON FATHER'S DAY

Every year on Father's Day, most people reflect on their father and their relationship with him. Fathering is a rigorous and exhausting job—even in the best of times. It is a time/labor intensive job that is often thankless. In this dark period of societal ignorance, fathering is exponentially complex and challenging.

Hopefully, traveling through the preceding chapters shines Light on your experience of fathering. With clarity, you can reclaim lost power. You can rescript your childhood and retool your internalized father-voice.

And supremely, you can provide a healthy family for your own children.

If you experienced toxic dad, you can find support and counseling to resolve childhood issues so they don't multiply in your family of creation. See the chapter *For Further Study* at the end of this book. There's a plethora of good books to help you. It is vitally important to reverse the reversed-wiring from your abusive childhood.

However, it is also useful to remember that we all are broken here on the earthly plane of duality. Brokenness comes with the birth certificate. The broken place is how the Light gets in.

Your father's greatest wound can become your deepest wisdom. We redeem power from the pain.

LOVE IS ETERNAL

The life your dad gave you is important. The love your dad gave you is also important. After you unwind the twisted vine of child abuse, you separate the toxic from the healthy love you received.

Over time and with wound repair, the toxic love dissipates. The healthy love remains. It is eternal. True love endures across lifetimes. Toxic love is transient. It subsides. True love's triumph is amazing. The good is bigger than the bad.

Even if your dad were a sperm donor, orgasm is a moment of God union. There is Divine Love in that moment—even in a sperm bank or a complex conception. His spark lit the way for you to find incarnation.

Most importantly, your dad gave you a ticket to ride the human experience. Gaining entrance here is a glorious privilege. He opened the door for you.

Fathers and Fathering

When you forgive your dad his humanness, you forgive yourself your humanness. You stop playing God. Instead of grandiosity and judgmentalness, you accept the limits of life. You accept your Soul Contract. You become a spiritual adult.

You forgive your dad for your own good. Resentment is too heavy a burden to carry. It can destroy you. Cutting the negative ties from the past frees you to go forward with your life.

Deeper than the right-wrong battles, it is worth remembering Hemingway's beautiful insight, "Love is infinitely more durable than hate." Forgiveness is the price of being human.

SPIRITUAL ADULTHOOD

This book is medicine. **Fathers and Fathering** helps you to digest and to process your childhood. It guides you to healthy selfhood, self-parenting, and correcting childhood mistakes. It provides skills to heal your childhood and internal voices.

This book teaches you healthy parenting skills to raise your children and to heal your internal self-talk. It illumines gender wars, this moment in history, and planetary confusion.

Fathers and Fathering invites you to your complete God Ladder, your Wise Man, your Wise Woman, and your holy family.

Families are where children learn healthy selfhood and leadership. Without healthy families, civilization can unspool. Healthy parenting is essential—both personally and globally.

Can we move from "me" to "we"—from power-games to co-creation, from arrested development to spiritual adulthood? Can we heal our broken family models? Can we embrace wisdom technologies?

The dialogue is between adult/child, male/female, mom/dad, earthly/divine energies. This conversation is inside each of us. Are we going to integrate and transcend—or, will we polarize?

Are we going to transcend selfishness to serve the good of the whole? Can we embrace deep gender-essence? Can we recalibrate twisted, gender social-roles? Will we embody the Wise

Fathers and Fathering

Man and Wise Woman?

My deep-dive into fathering opened gender-avenues that I never expected to travel. My exploration gave me life skills, self-awareness, awakenings, and divine dispensations. It gave me my beloved, wise husband and the God Ladder. I am eternally grateful for the Wisdom Way. It saves my sanity every day!

The great spiritual teacher Neem Karoli Baba says, "Love everyone. Serve everyone. Remember God." That's the Wisdom Way. It sounds simple, but it isn't easy. Endless humility and great warriorship is required as you journey to the Sacred Feet.

As a grandmother, I invite you to step forward into ownership of your complete self. Claim your divine birthright to wholeness. Stand in the greatness of your Wise Man and your Wise Woman.

The soul calls to each of us saying,

> *Dear Human Child,*
>
> *Rise up! You walk as gods and goddesses on earth. Wear your crown wisely. Don't waste your opportunity.*
>
> *Join God's Army! Stand shoulder to shoulder with Wisdom Keepers across the globe. Claim your Wise Man and your Wise Woman. Embody your divine birthright to walk in the Wisdom Way.*
>
> *The planet is yours. Hold it in your arms. Nurture and embrace it. Speak your truth. Work together with others. Heal the broken places.*
>
> *The future is in your hands. The medicine is yours.*

Honoring the soul within each of us empowers the Sacred Feminine, so needed for balance in today's world. Divine Mother loves, nurtures, and guides the child. She restores conscience and healthy limits. She heals psychological and social imbalances of grandiosity, abuse, and action addiction.

Wielding power in service to the whole honors the Sacred Masculine. Divine Father brings divine truth, ego transcension, and justice.

The Sacred Path creates the Sacred Human necessary for the Human Experiment to evolve. The Wisdom Keeper embraces both heaven and earth; the duality and the divine; male and female; yours and mine—simultaneously.

The Wise One lives with indwelling bliss even while immersed in the imperfect, messy, always changing, limited, earthly duality. The Wisdom Keeper experiences a lifestyle of consecration, knowing each day as an altar. The Wisdom Way trusts the divine plan behind earthly events.

With participatory divinity, the Wisdom Keeper experiences blessed ordinariness and living in the amazement of this wondrous earth-ride. The Wise One rejoices in small things, seeing life as a magic-show, and taking nothing for granted.

Amidst the wrestling and wrangling of daily life, the Wisdom Warrior lives imperfectly, while taking great joy in the beauty here. The Wise One knows that life is a gift and is humbly grateful.

Anchoring the Wisdom Keeper is the current invitation in the evolution of the Human Experiment. The Divine Light needs earthly embodiment at this important time. The New Wisdom Age needs the Wise Man and the Wise Woman.

I stand with you in claiming your victory. You have the medicine!

FOR FURTHER STUDY

ON MEN

Bly, Robert. *Iron John: A Book about Men.* NY, NY: Addison-Wesley Publishing, 1990.

Carter, Steven. *Men Who Can't Love.* NY, NY: Berkley Books, 1987.

Farrell, Warren. *The Myth of Male Power.* NY, NY: Berkley Books, 1993.

Farrell, Warren. *Why Men Are the Way They Are.* NY, NY: Berkley Books, 1987.

Goldberg, Herb. *The Hazards of Being Male: Surviving the Myth of Masculine Privilege.* NY, NY: Signet Books, 1976.

Keen, Sam. *Fire in the Belly: On Being a Man.* NY, NY: Bantam Books, 1991.

Kiley, Dan. *The Peter Pan Syndrome: Men Who Have Never Grown Up.* NY, NY: Avon Books, 1983.

Lee, John. *The Flying Boy: Healing the Wounded Man.* Deerfield, FL: Health Communications, 1987.

Reno, Judith Larkin. *Fathers and Fathering: An Exploration.* Vista, CA: Gateway University, 2013.

ON RELATIONSHIPS

Anonymous. *One Day at a Time in Al Anon.* NY: Al-Anon Family Group Headquarters, 1973.

Anonymous. *The Courage to Change.* NY: Al-Anon Family Group Headquarters, 1992.

Beatty, Melodie. *Beyond Codependency.* NY: Harper & Row, 1989.

Bloomfield, Harold, and Sirah Vettese. *Life-Mates: The Love Fitness Program for a Lasting Relationship.* NY: Signet, 1989.

Bradshaw, John. *Creating Love: The Next Great Stage of Growth.* NY, NY: Bantam, 1994.

----------. *Bradshaw: On the Family.*

Brandon, Nathaniel. *The Psychology of Romantic Love.* NY: Bantam, 1981.

Buber, Martin. *I and Thou.* NY: Charles Scribner, 1958.

Chia, Mantak and Maneewan Chia. *Healing Love Through the Tao: Cultivating Female Sexual Energy.* Huntington, NY: Healing Tao Books, 1992.

Chia, Mantak. *Taoist Secrets of Love: Cultivating Male Sexual Energy.* NY, NY: Aurora Press, 1986.

De Angelis, Barbara. *Making Love Work: Personal Guidebook.* Baltimore, MD: Inphomation, Inc., 1993.

Evat, Cris. *He and She: 60 Significant Differences between Men and Women.* Berkeley, CA: Conari Press, 1992.

Farrell, Warren. *Why Men Are the Way They Are.* NY: Berkley, 1988.

--------. *The Myth of Male Power.*

Gilligan, Carol. *In a Different Voice: Psychological Theory and Women's Development.* Cambridge, MA: Harvard University Press, 1982.

Glass, Lillian. *Toxic People: 10 Ways of Dealing with People Who Make Your Life Miserable.* NY: Simon & Schuster, 1995.

Fathers and Fathering

Goldberg, Herb. *The Hazards of Being Male: Surviving the Myth of Masculine Privilege.* NY: Signet, 1976.

Gray, John. *Men Are from Mars, Women Are from Venus: A Practical Guide for Improving Communication and Getting What You Want in Your Relationships.* NY, NY: Harper Collins, 1992.

----------. *Men, Women and Relationships: Making Peace with the Opposite Sex.* Hillsboro, OR: Beyond Words Publishing, 1990.

----------. *What Your Mother Couldn't Tell You & Your Father Didn't Know. Advanced Relationship Skills for Better Communication and Lasting Intimacy.* NY: Harper Collins, 1994.

Hendricks, Gay, and Kathllyn Hendricks. *Conscious Loving: The Journey to Co-Commitment.* NY: Bantam, 1992.

Hendrix, Harville. *Getting the Love You Want: A Guide for Couples.* NY: Harper Perennial, 1988.

----------. *Keeping the Love You Find.* NY: Pocket Books, 1992.

----------, and Helen Hunt. *The Couples Companion: Meditations and Exercises for Getting the Love You Want.* NY: Pocket Books, 1994.

Johnson, Robert A. *Femininity Lost and Regained.* NY: Harper & Row, 1990.

----------. *He.*

----------. *She: Understanding Feminine Psychology.* NY: Harper & Row, 1977.

----------. *We: Understanding the Psychology of Romantic Love.* San Francisco, CA: Harper & Row, 1983.

Keen, Sam. *Fire in the Belly: On Being a Man.* NY: Bantam, 1991.

Kiley, Dan. *The Peter Pan Syndrome: Men Who Have Never Grown Up.* NY: Avon, 1983.

Kipnis, Aaron, and Elizabeth Herron. *Gender War, Gender Peace.* NY, NY: William Morrow, 1994.

Kriesman, Jerold, and Hal Straus. *I Hate You, Don't Leave Me: Understanding the Borderline Personality.* LA: The Body Press, 1989.

Lee, John. *The Flying Boy: Why Men Run from Relationships.* Deerfield Beach, FLA: Health Communications, 1987.

Lerner, Harriet. *The Dance of Anger: A Woman's Guide to Changing the Patterns of Intimate Relationships.* NY: Harper & Row, 1986.

Levine, Stephen and Ondrea. *Embracing the Beloved: Relationship as a Path of Awakening.* NY, NY: Doubleday, 1994.

Prather, Hugh, and Gayle. *A Book for Couples.* NY: Bantam Doubleday, 1988.

Reno, Judith Larkin. *A Mystic's View of War: Using the God Ladder for Clarity.* Philadelphia, PA: Xlibris, 2002.

--------. *Elephants in Your Tent: Spiritual Support as a Mystic Survives Cancer.* Philadelphia, PA: Xlibris, 2005.

--------. *Healing the Broken Family: Skills for Renewal and Insight.* Vista, CA: Gateway University, 2012.

--------. *Love is Made: The How-To Love Manual.* Vista, CA: Gateway University, 2012.

--------. *Love's Triumph: Child-Abuse Recovery with Soul Support.* Vista, CA: Gateway University, 2009.

--------. *The Lightening Years: Menopause as Spiritual Initiation.* Vista, CA: Gateway University, 2012.

--------. *The God Ladder. Spiritual Initiation for Living Now.* Vista, CA: Gateway University, 2005.

--------. *New Year Sacred Celebration: Find Your New Soul-Path.* Vista, CA: Gateway University, 2009.

--------. *Valentine's Day Sacred Celebration: The Deep Meaning of Love and Sex.* Vista, CA: Gateway University, 2009.

--------. *Easter Sacred Celebration: Holy City Initiation.* Vista, CA: Gateway University, 2009.

--------. *Mother's Day Sacred Celebration: The Divine Mother.* Vista, CA: Gateway University, 2009.

--------. *Fathers and Fathering: An Exploration.* Vista, CA: Gateway University, 2012.

--------. *Christmas Sacred Celebration: The Midnight Angel Procession.* Vista, CA: Gateway University, 2009.

--------. *Your Home Sacred Celebration: Your Home Angel.* Vista, CA: Gateway University, 2009.

--------. *Your Birthday Sacred Celebration: Find Your Soul-Path for Each Year.* Vista, CA: Gateway University, 2009.

--------. *The Gateway Weekly Workout: Pump 'n Tone Your Spirituality.* Vista, CA: Gateway University, 2009.

--------. *The Signature Wedding: Design Your Own Wedding Ceremony.* Vista, CA: Gateway University, 2009.

Richo, David. *How To Be an Adult: A Handbook on Psychological and Spiritual Integration.* NY: Paulist Press, 1991.

Tanenbaum, Joe. *Male and Female Realities: Understanding the Opposite Sex.* San Marcos, CA: Robert Erdmann Publishing, 1991.

Tannen, Deborah. *You Just Don't Understand: Women and Men in Conversation.* NY, NY: Ballantine, 1990.

Vessell, Barry, and Joyce. *The Shared Heart.* Aptos, CA: Ramira Publishing, 1984.

Wallerstein, Judith, and Sandra Blakeslee. *Second Chances: Men, Women, and Children After Divorce.* NY: Ticknor and Fields, 1989.

Welwood, John. *Journey of the Heart: Intimate Relationship and the Path of Love.* NY: Harper Perennial, 1992.

Weiner-Davis, Michele. *Divorce Busting: Marriage-Saving Tips that Work.* NY, NY: Simon Schuster, Fireside, 1993.

ON FAMILY

Ackerman, Robert, and Susan Pickering. *Abused No More: Recovery for Women in Abusive and/or Codependent Alcoholic Relationships.* Blue Ridge Summin, PA: TAB Books, 1989.

Arterburn Stephen. *Addicted to Love: Recovery from Unhealthy Dependency in Love, Romantic Relationships and Sex.* Ann Arbor, MI: Servant Publications, 1991.

Bandler, Leslie. *They Lived Happily Ever After.* Cupertino, CA: Meta Publications, 1978.

Bach, George, and Peter Wyden. *The Intimate Enemy: How to Fight Fair in Love and Marriage.* NY: Avon Books, 1970.

Bandler, Richard, and Grinder, John. *Frogs into Princes.* Moab, UT: Real People Press, 1979.

----------. *Reframing.* . Moab, UT: Real People Press, 1982.

Bass, Ellen, and Davis, Laura. *The Courage to Heal: A Guide for Women Survivors of Child Sexual Abuse.* NY, NY: Harper & Row, 1994.

Bireda, Martha. *Love Addiction: A Guide to Emotional Independence.* Oakland, CA: New Harbinger, 1990.

Beattie, Melody. *Codependent No More: How to Stop Controlling Others and Start Caring for Yourself.*

----------. *Beyond Codependency.* NY: Harper & Row, 1989.

----------. *Codependents' Guide to the Twelve Steps.* NY: A Fireside/Parkside Recovery Book, Simon & Schuster, 1990.

Berne, Eric. *Games People Play: The Basic Handbook of Transactional Analysis.* NY: Ballantine, 1978.

----------. *What Do You Say After You Say Hello?* NY: Bantam, 1982.

Bly, Robert. *Iron Man.* Redding, MA: Addison-Wesley, 1990.

Bowen, Murray. *Family Therapy in Clinical Practice.* Northvale, NJ: Jason Aronson, 1978.

Bradshaw, John. *Bradshaw On: The Family: A Revolutionary Way of Self-Discovery.*

----------. *Homecoming: Reclaiming and Championing Your Inner Child.*

----------. *Creating Love: The Next Great Stage of Growth.* NY, NY: Bantam, 1994.

----------. *Bradshaw On: Healing the Shame that Binds You.* Deerfield Beach, FLA: 1988.

Fathers and Fathering

Burns, David. *The Feeling Good Handbook.* NY: Penguin, 1989.

----------. *Feeling Good: The New Mood Therapy.*

----------. *When Panic Attacks: The New, Drug-Free Anxiety Therapy That Can Change Your Life.* NY: Broadway Books, 2006.

Carnes, Patrick. *Out of the Shadows.* Irvine, CA: CompCare Pub, 1985.

----------. *Contrary to Love.* Irvine, CA: CompCare Publishers, 1988.

Clarke, Jean Illsley. *Self-Esteem: A Family Affair.* NY: Harper & Row, 1980.

----------, and Dawson, Connie. *Growing Up Again.* NY: Harper & Row, 1989.

Covington, Stephanie. *Leaving the Enchanted Forest: The Path from Relationship Addiction.* San Francisco, CA: HarperSanFrancisco, 1988.

Covitz, Joel. *Emotional Child Abuse.* Boston, MA: Sigo Press, 1986.

Dowling, Collette, *The Cinderella Complex: Women's Hidden Fear of Independence.* NY: Pocketbooks, 1981.

Dreikurs, Rudolf, and Vick Stolz. *Children, The Challenge.* NY, NY: Dutton, 1987.

Erickson, Milton. *Childhood and Society.* NY: W. W. Norton, 1950.

Firestone, Robert. *The Fantasy Bond: Effects of Psychological Defenses on Interpersonal Relationships.* NY, NY: Human Sciences Press, 1985.

Forward, Susan. *Toxic Parents.* NY: Bantam Books, 1989.

Foster, Carolyn. *The Family Patterns Workbook.*

Fromm, Erich. *The Art of Loving.* NY, NY: Harper Collins, 1989.

----------. *The Heart of Man.* NY: Harper & Row, 1964.

Glass, Lillian. *Toxic People: 10 Ways of Dealing with People Who Make Your Life Miserable.* NY: Simon & Schuster, 1995.

Gorski, Terence T. *The Players and Their Personalities: Understanding the People Who Get Involved in Addictive Relationships.* Independence, MO: Herald House, 1989.

Gordon, Thomas. *Parent Effectiveness Training.* NY, NY: McKay, 1970.

Harris, Thomas. *I'm OK--You're OK: Transactional Analysis Breakthrough Helping People Who Never Felt OK About Themselves.* NY: Avon, 1973.

Hemfelt, Minirth, and Meier. *Love is a Choice: Recovery for Codependent Relationships.*

Hendricks, Gay. *Learning to Love Yourself.* Englewood Cliffs, NJ: Prentice Hall.

Hoffman, Bob. *No One is to Blame.* Palo Alto, CA: Science and Behavior, 1979.

Horney, Karen. *Neurosis and Human Growth.* NY: W. W. Norton & Co., 1970.

Imbach, Jeff. *The Recovery of Love: Christian Mysticism and the Addictive Society.* NY: The Crossroad Publishing, 1991.

Jackson, Don, and William Lederer. *The Mirages of Marriage.* NY, NY: W.W. Norton & Co, 1968.

Johnson, Robert. *Owning Your Shadow.* San Francisco, CA: Harper, 1991.

Johnson, Robert A. *Femininity Lost and Regained.* NY: Harper & Row, 1990.

----------. *She: Understanding Feminine Psychology.* NY: Harper & Row, 1977.

----------. *He: Understanding Male Psychology.* NY: Harper & Row.

----------. *We: Understanding the Psychology of Romantic Love.* San Francisco, CA: Harper & Row, 1983.

Jung, Carl. *Four Archetypes.* Princeton, NJ: Princeton University Press, 1985.

----------. *Memories, Dreams, Reflections.* NY: Random House, 1989.

----------. *Collected Works.*

Kaufman, Gershen. *The Psychology of Shame.* NY: Springer Pub, 1989.

Fathers and Fathering

Keen, Sam. *Fire in the Belly.* NY: Bantam, 1991.

Kriesman, Jerold, and Hal Straus. *I Hate You, Don't Leave Me: Understanding the Borderline Personality.* LA: The Body Press, 1989.

Laing, R. D. *The Divided Self.* NY: Viking Penguin, 1968.

Lee, John H. *I Don't Want To Be Alone: For Men and Women Who Want to Heal Addictive Relationships.* Deerfield, FL: Healthy Communications, 1990.

Leman, Kevin. *The Birth Order Book: Why You Are the Way You Are.* NY: Dell, 1985.

Lerner, Harriet. *The Dance of Anger: A Woman's Guide to Changing the Patterns of Intimate Relationships.* NY: Harper & Row, 1986.

----------. *The Dance of Intimacy.* NY: Harper & Row, 1989.

Love, Patricia. *The Emotional Incest Syndrome: What to do When a Parent's Love Rules Your Life.* NY: Bantam, 1990.

Mason, Paul T. and Randi Kreger. *Stop Walking on Eggshells: Taking Back Your Life When Someone You Care About Has Borderline Personality Disorder.* Oakland, CA: New Harbinger, 1998.

Mellody, Pia. *Facing Codependence: What It Is, Where It Comes From, How It Sabotages Our Lives.* San Francisco, CA: HarperSanFrancisco, 1989.

---------- *Facing Love Addiction: Giving Yourself the Power to Change the Way You Love.* San Francisco, CA: HarperSanFrancisco, 1992.

----------, and Andrew Wells Miller. *Breaking Free: A Workbook for Facing Codependence.* San Francisco, CA: HarperSanFrancisco, 1989.

Miller, Alice. *For Your Own Good.* NY: Farrar, Straus, & Giroux, 1983.

----------. *The Drama of the Gifted Child.*

----------. *Banished Knowledge.*

----------. *Pictures of Childhood.*

Norwood, Robin. *Women Who Love Too Much.* NY: St Martin's Press, 1985.

Peele, Stanton, and Brodsky, Archie. *Love and Addiction.* NY: Signet, New American Library, 1987.

Pelletier, Ken. *Mind as Healer, Mind as Slayer.* NY: Delta/Dell, 1977.

Perls, Fritz. *Gestalt Therapy Verbatim.* Moab, UT: Real People Press, 1969.

Reno, Judith Larkin. *A Mystic's View of War: Using the God Ladder for Clarity.* Philadelphia, PA: Xlibris, 2002.

--------. *Elephants in Your Tent: Spiritual Support as a Mystic Survives Cancer.* Philadelphia, PA: Xlibris, 2005.

--------. *Healing the Broken Family: Skills for Renewal and Insight.* Vista, CA: Gateway University, 2012.

--------. *The Lightening Years: Menopause as Spiritual Initiation.* Vista, CA: Gateway University, 2012.

--------. *Love is Made: The How-To Love Manual.* Vista, CA: Gateway University, 2012.

--------. *Love's Triumph: Child-Abuse Recovery with Soul Support.* Vista, CA: Gateway University, 2009.

--------. *The Signature Wedding: Design Your Own Wedding Ceremony.* Vista, CA: Gateway University, 2009.

--------. *New Year Sacred Celebration: Find Your New Soul-Path.* Vista, CA: Gateway University, 2009.

--------. *Valentine's Day Sacred Celebration: The Deep Meaning of Love and Sex.* Vista, CA: Gateway University, 2009.

--------. *Easter Sacred Celebration: Holy City Initiation.* Vista, CA: Gateway University, 2009.

--------. *Mother's Day Sacred Celebration: The Divine Mother.* Vista, CA: Gateway University, 2009.

--------. *Fathers and Fathering: An Exploration.* Vista, CA: Gateway University, 2012.

———. *Spiritual Initiation and The Christmas Angel Procession.* Vista, CA: Gateway University, 2013.

———. *Spiritual Initiation: The Seven Gateways.* Vista, CA: Gateway University, 2013.

———. *Christmas Sacred Celebration: The Midnight Angel Procession.* Vista, CA: Gateway University, 2009.

———. *The Christmas Angel Procession.* Vista, CA: Gateway University, 2012.

———. *Your Home Sacred Celebration: Your Home Angel.* Vista, CA: Gateway University, 2009.

———. *Your Birthday Sacred Celebration: Find Your Soul-Path for Each Year.* Vista, CA: Gateway University, 2009.

———. *The Gateway Weekly Workout: Pump 'n Tone Your Spirituality.* Vista, CA: Gateway University, 2009.

———. *The God Ladder. Spiritual Initiation for Living Now.* Vista, CA: Gateway University, 2005.

———. *Divine Father—Your God: Deepening Your God Connection.* Vista, CA: Gateway University, 2010.

———. *Divine Mother—Your Soul: Deepening Your Soul Connection.* Vista, CA: Gateway University, 2010.

———. *Reinventing God: God Discovery—Personally and Historically.* Vista, CA: Gateway University, 2010.

———. *Self-Interview: Using Your God Ladder for Self-Discovery.* Vista, CA: Gateway University, 2010.

Rogers, Carl. *On Becoming a Person.* Boston, MA: Houghton Mifflin, 1972.

Sanford, Linda. *Strong at the Broken Places: Overcoming the Trauma of Childhood Abuse.* NY: Avon Books, 1992.

Satir, Virginia. *Conjoint Family Therapy.* Palo Alto, CA: Science and Behavior, 1982.

Schaef, Anne Wilson. *Escape from Intimacy: Untangling Love Addictions: Sex, Romance, Relationships.* San Francisco, CA: HarperSanFrancisco, 1990.

----------. *Codependence: Misunderstood, Mistreated.* Minneapolis, MN: Winston Press, 1987.

----------. *When Society Becomes an Addict.* San Francisco, CA: Harper & Row, 1987.

Shengold, Leonard. *Soul Murder: The Effects of Childhood Abuse and Deprivation.* New Haven, NJ: Yale University Press, 1989.

Smith, Manuel. *When I Say No, I Feel Guilty.* NY: Bantam

Steiner, Claude. *Scripts People Live: Transactional Analysis of Life Scripts.* NY: Bantam, 1972.

Stone, Hal, and Sidra Winkelman. *Embracing Ourselves.* Marina del Rey, CA: Devors Publishing.

Taylor, Cathryn. *The Inner Child Workbook: What To Do with Your Past When It Just Won't Go Away.* NY: Jeremy Tarcher, 1993.

Viorst, Judith. *Necessary Losses.* NY: Simon & Schuster.

Wegscheider-Cruse, Sharon. *Choicemaking.* Pompano Beach, FLA: Health Communications, 1985.

----------. *Learning to Love Yourself.* Pompano Beach, FLA: Health Communications, 1987.

Weiner-Davis, Michele. *Divorce Busting: Marriage-Saving Tips that Work.* NY, NY: Simon Schuster, Fireside, 1993.

Weinhold, Barry. *Breaking Free of Addictive Family Relationships.* Dallas, TX: Stillpoint, 1991.

Whitfield, Charles. *Boundaries and Relationships: Knowing, Protecting, and Enjoying the Self.* . Pompano Beach, FLA: Health Communications.

----------. *Healing the Child Within.* . Pompano Beach, FLA: Health Communications, 1987.

----------. *Codependence: Healing the Human Condition.*

Woititz, Janet. *Adult-Children of Alcoholics.* . Pompano Beach, FLA: Health Communications.

----------. *Struggle for Intimacy.* . Pompano Beach, FLA: Health Communications.

Woodman, Marion. *Addiction to Perfection.* Toronto: Inner City Books, 1982.

Zukav, Gary. *The Seat of the Soul.* NY: Simon & Schuster, 1989.

AUDIOS

See www.GatewayUniversity.org. for the following recommended audios with Rev. Dr. Judith Larkin Reno in the Gateway University Wisdom Collection:

➢ Father's Day Sacred Celebration: The Father Archetype
➢ The First Father's Day
➢ Why Did God Create the Experience of Fathering?

www.ingramcontent.com/pod-product-compliance
Lightning Source LLC
Chambersburg PA
CBHW031141160426
43193CB00008B/213